Digital Forensics with Kali Linux

Perform data acquisition, digital investigation, and threat analysis using Kali Linux tools

Shiva V.N. Parasram

BIRMINGHAM - MUMBAI

Digital Forensics with Kali Linux

Copyright © 2017 Packt Publishing

First published: December 2017

Production reference: 1151217

Published by Packt Publishing Ltd.
Livery Place
35 Livery Street
Birmingham
B3 2PB, UK.
ISBN 978-1-78862-500-5

www.packtpub.com

Credits

Author
Shiva V.N. Parasram

Reviewers
Alex Samm
Dale Joseph

Commissioning Editor
Gebin George

Acquisition Editor
Rahul Nair

Content Development Editor
Nithin Varghese

Technical Editor
Vishal Kamal Mewada

Copy Editor
Safis Editing

Project Coordinator
Virginia Dias

Proofreader
Safis Editing

Indexer
Rekha Nair

Production Coordinator
Melwyn Dsa

Disclaimer

The information within this book is intended to be used only in an ethical manner. Do not use any information from the book if you do not have written permission from the owner of the equipment. If you perform illegal actions, you are likely to be arrested and prosecuted to the full extent of the law. Packt Publishing does not take any responsibility if you misuse any of the information contained within the book. The information herein must only be used while testing environments with proper written authorizations from appropriate persons responsible.

About the Author

Shiva V.N. Parasram is an IT and cybersecurity professional with 13 years of experience in IT security and over 5 years in penetration testing and digital forensics investigations and training. Some of his qualifications include an MSc. in Network Security (Distinction), CEH, CHFI, ECSA, CEI, CCNA, ACE, and NSE. Having been the Director and CISO of his own company, the Computer Forensics and Security Institute (CFSI), since 2011, he has carried out investigations and pentesting for some of the largest private companies in the Caribbean. As a Certified EC-Council Instructor (CEI), he has also trained many people in the banking and private sectors, the Ministry of National Security, and protective services in Trinidad and Tobago, and also lectures in digital forensics at the postgraduate level.

Being a cyber-security and forensics lecturer at heart, I've always loved sharing my knowledge and creating labs and tutorials, hoping to someday have them all published. Needless to say, I was nothing short of elated when Rahul Nair of Packt Publishing contacted me and offered me the amazing opportunity to write this book.

Many thanks to everyone who made the publishing of this book possible. To my Packt family, including my technical editor Vishal Mewada and editor and friend, Nithin George Varghese, for all his encouragement, especially at times when I was completely overwhelmed and needed those many motivational talks. To my cheerleaders at work, Heather Ali and Deborah Romero, who would pick up lunch for me on a daily basis and encourage me to use my lunch hour to further my research. My brilliant technical reviewers, Mr. Dale Joseph at the National CyberCrime Unit and Mr. Alex Samm, the international Sys. Admin. himself at ESP Global. Special thanks to Bepnesh Goolcharran of Tier10 Technologies and Mr. Glen Singh of XyberFusion Ltd. for their exceptional research assistance at all hours of the evening, including at weekends.

To my MSc Lecturer, Mr. Vishal Ramnarine, for all his support and encouragement in pushing me to always give my best and rise to the top.

Special thanks to my dear Guru Pt. Hardeo Persad, my friends Dr. Mala Maharaj, Dr. Nirvan Basdeo, and my dear Dr. Hari Maharajh, who helped me get here and will forever live in my heart and memory.

Finally, to my very loving, supportive, and fun family, Harry G. and Indra Parasram, Nalini and Ravi Rajballie, Aneela Mahabir and Aarav (the minion), and of course Vaani. Thank you all so much for your patience, love, and support. You are my light after the long night and my greatest blessings. I love you all very much. Thank you all.

About the Reviewers

Dale Joseph is a digital forensic expert with over 9 years of experience in high technology investigations in Trinidad and Tobago. He has over 19 years of law enforcement and fraud investigative experience and has been involved in numerous high-profile technology-based investigations. Dale is the cofounder of DTECTT Digital Forensics Limited, which was formed to address the need for technology-based investigations, e-discovery, and cybersecurity in the private sector of Trinidad and Tobago. Currently, he performs the role of the company's senior technical consultant. His areas of expertise include the following:

- Wireless and VOIP investigations
- Investigative scripting
- Open source and internet investigations
- Network forensics
- Computer forensics
- Live data forensics
- Mobile forensics
- Malware investigations

Dale holds a BSc in computer science from the University of Hertfordshire, England, and an MSc in forensic computing and cyber crime investigations from University College Dublin, Ireland. He has attended several digital forensics/cyber crime investigation training courses in the United States, Europe, the Caribbean, and Latin America. Dale is also a certified digital forensics trainer and has conducted several workshops/seminars that have trained members of law enforcement, the private sector, and government entities in Trinidad and Tobago in the areas of technology-based investigations, cyber security, and internet safety. He has collaborated with law enforcement agencies in the Caribbean and Latin America regarding cyber crime investigations. Dale loves to travel and is an avid reader; he is also a huge fan of reggae music and good food, particularly Chinese and Caribbean cuisine.

My contribution to this book is dedicated to my father Steve; you have always been my motivation to succeed, you were always there to support me. I miss you dad, rest in peace.

Alex Samm has over 10 years of experience in the IT field, including system and network administration, end user computing support, Windows and Linux server support, virtualization, programming, penetration testing, and forensic investigations. Currently, he provides his services to ESP Global Services, providing support for many contracts including airlines and airports, pharmaceutical companies, and others. This primarily covers North America, Latin America, and the Caribbean. He also lectures at the Computer Forensics and Security Institute on IT security courses, including ethical hacking and penetration testing.

www.PacktPub.com

For support files and downloads related to your book, please visit www.PacktPub.com.

Did you know that Packt offers eBook versions of every book published, with PDF and ePub files available? You can upgrade to the eBook version at www.PacktPub.com, and as a print book customer, you are entitled to a discount on the eBook copy. Get in touch with us at service@packtpub.com for more details.

At www.PacktPub.com, you can also read a collection of free technical articles, sign up for a range of free newsletters and receive exclusive discounts and offers on Packt books and eBooks.

https://www.packtpub.com/mapt

Get the most in-demand software skills with Mapt. Mapt gives you full access to all Packt books and video courses, as well as industry-leading tools to help you plan your personal development and advance your career.

Why subscribe?

- Fully searchable across every book published by Packt
- Copy and paste, print, and bookmark content
- On demand and accessible via a web browser

Customer Feedback

Thanks for purchasing this Packt book. At Packt, quality is at the heart of our editorial process. To help us improve, please leave us an honest review on this book's Amazon page at https://www.amazon.com/dp/1788625005.

If you'd like to join our team of regular reviewers, you can email us at customerreviews@packtpub.com. We award our regular reviewers with free eBooks and videos in exchange for their valuable feedback. Help us be relentless in improving our products!

Table of Contents

Preface

In today's world, new threats, breaches, and malicious activities are discovered and published in the news, websites, and portals quite regularly. As much as we try to secure our data, systems, and networks to the best of our abilities, breaches occur. In an effort to understand what took place, we turn to the field of digital forensics. Although still a relatively new field, forensics has become just as important as security, especially when considering the wealth of information available to anyone accessing the internet with the intent of carrying out malicious activity. Thankfully, digital fingerprints and artifacts are sometimes left behind, whether in a deleted or hidden file, email, in someone's browsing history, remote connection list, or even mobile text message.

This book gives even the absolute beginner a structured approach with best practices to carry out their own investigations using the popular and powerful forensics tools in Kali Linux, many of which are used by military organizations and forensic investigators worldwide.

What this book covers

Chapter 1, *Introduction to Digital Forensics*, gives an introduction to the various aspects of the science of digital forensics.

Chapter 2, *Installing Kali Linux*, shows how to we install, configure, and update Kali Linux. The installation process will be followed on both physical and virtual machines to the benefit of users with both single and multiple machines for running Kali Linux. Once installed, we explore the Forensics menu in Kali Linux.

Chapter 3, *Understanding Filesystems and Storage Media*, dives into the realm of operating systems and the various formats for file storage, including secret hiding places not seen by the end user or even the operating system. We also inspect data about the data, known as metadata, and look at its volatility.

Chapter 4, *Incident Response and Data Acquisition*, asks what happens when an incident is reported or detected? Who are the first responders and what are the procedures for maintaining the integrity of the evidence? In this chapter, we look at best practices and procedures in data acquisition and evidence collection.

Chapter 5, *Evidence Acquisition and Preservation with DC3DD and Guymager*, focuses on one of the most important aspects of forensic acquisition. Learn to create forensic images of data and maintain integrity using hashing tools.

Chapter 6, *File Recovery and Data Carving with Foremost, Scalpel, and Bulk Extractor*, states that data disappears, whether accidentally, intentionally, or just hidden from plain sight and the operating system. In this chapter, we look at two powerful tools used to perform file recovery and learn about advanced search features.

Chapter 7, *Memory Forensics with Volatility*, states that in today's digital world we sometimes encounter scenarios that require the use of live memory forensics. Learn to use this powerful memory forensics tool to view running processes, programs, and live artifacts.

Chapter 8, *Autopsy – The Sleuth Kit*, introduces Autopsy which is recognized as one of the very few available tools to rival commercial forensic tools, this powerful tool takes forensic abilities and investigations to a professional level, catering for all aspects of full digital forensics investigations from hashing to reporting.

Chapter 9, *Network and Internet Capture Analysis with Xplico*, investigates and analyzes captured network and internet traffic using this powerful tool.

Chapter 10, *Revealing Evidence Using DFF*, shows how two tools are better than one. Use another advanced forensic framework tool to carry out full and professional digital forensics investigations, ensuring the integrity of your findings by comparing the results found.

What you need for this book

To follow the exercises in this book, readers will need to download the following:

- Kali Linux 2017.2 x64 and Kali Linux 2017.1 x64
- VirtualBox 5.2 or higher
- Kali Linux 2017.2 burnt to a DVD

Who this book is for

This book is intended for network, systems, and security administrators; information security officers; auditors; IT managers; and also students, researchers, security enthusiasts, and anyone interested in the field of digital forensics or interested in learning about specific tools for various stages of investigations, from evidence acquisition and preservation to analysis, using powerful forensic suites.

Conventions

In this book, you will find a number of text styles that distinguish between different kinds of information. Here are some examples of these styles and an explanation of their meaning. Code words in the text, database table names, folder names, filenames, file extensions, pathnames, dummy URLs, user input, and Twitter handles are shown as follows: "To begin installing DFF, we first need to update the `sources.list` with the repository used in Kali Sana."

A block of code is set as follows:

```
deb http://http.kali.org/kali kali-rolling main contrib non-free
deb src http://http.kali.org/kali kali-rolling main contrib non-
free
deb http://http.kali.org/kali sana main contrib
```

When we wish to draw your attention to a particular part of a code block, the relevant lines or items are set in bold:

```
deb http://http.kali.org/kali kali-rolling main contrib non-free
deb src http://http.kali.org/kali kali-rolling main contrib non-
free
deb http://http.kali.org/kali sana main contrib
```

Any command-line input or output is written as follows:

```
dc3dd if=/dev/sdb hash=sha1 log=dd_split_usb ofsz=500M
ofs=split_test_usb.img.ooo
```

New terms and **important words** are shown in bold.

Warnings or important notes appear like this.

Tips and tricks appear like this.

Reader feedback

Feedback from our readers is always welcome. Let us know what you think about this book-what you liked or disliked. Reader feedback is important to us as it helps us develop titles that you will really get the most out of. To send us general feedback, simply email feedback@packtpub.com, and mention the book's title in the subject of your message. If there is a topic that you have expertise in and you are interested in either writing or contributing to a book, see our author guide at www.packtpub.com/authors.

Customer support

Now that you are the proud owner of a Packt book, we have a number of things to help you to get the most from your purchase.

Downloading the example code

You can download the example code files for this book from your account at http://www.packtpub.com. If you purchased this book elsewhere, you can visit http://www.packtpub.com/support and register to have the files e-mailed directly to you. You can download the code files by following these steps:

1. Log in or register to our website using your e-mail address and password.
2. Hover the mouse pointer on the **SUPPORT** tab at the top.
3. Click on **Code Downloads & Errata**.
4. Enter the name of the book in the **Search** box.
5. Select the book for which you're looking to download the code files.

6. Choose from the drop-down menu where you purchased this book from.
7. Click on **Code Download**.

Once the file is downloaded, please make sure that you unzip or extract the folder using the latest version of:

- WinRAR / 7-Zip for Windows
- Zipeg / iZip / UnRarX for Mac
- 7-Zip / PeaZip for Linux

The code bundle for the book is also hosted on GitHub at `https://github.com/PacktPublishing/Digital-Forensics-with-Kali-Linux`. We also have other code bundles from our rich catalog of books and videos available at `https://github.com/PacktPublishing/`. Check them out!

Errata

Although we have taken every care to ensure the accuracy of our content, mistakes do happen. If you find a mistake in one of our books—maybe a mistake in the text or the code—we would be grateful if you could report this to us. By doing so, you can save other readers from frustration and help us improve subsequent versions of this book. If you find any errata, please report them by visiting `http://www.packtpub.com/submit-errata`, selecting your book, clicking on the Errata Submission Form link, and entering the details of your errata. Once your errata are verified, your submission will be accepted and the errata will be uploaded to our website or added to any list of existing errata under the Errata section of that title. To view the previously submitted errata, go to `https://www.packtpub.com/books/content/support`, and enter the name of the book in the search field. The required information will appear under the Errata section.

Piracy

Piracy of copyrighted material on the internet is an ongoing problem across all media. At Packt, we take the protection of our copyright and licenses very seriously. If you come across any illegal copies of our works in any form on the internet, please provide us with the location address or website name immediately so that we can pursue a remedy. Please contact us at `copyright@packtpub.com` with a link to the suspected pirated material. We appreciate your help in protecting our authors and our ability to bring you valuable content.

Questions

If you have a problem with any aspect of this book, you can contact us at
questions@packtpub.com, and we will do our best to address the problem.

1
Introduction to Digital Forensics

Digital forensics has had my attention for well over 13 years. Ever since I was given my first PC (thanks, Mom and Dad), I've always wondered what happened when I deleted my files from my massively large 2 GB hard drive or moved (and most times hid) my files to a less-than-inconspicuous 3.5-inch floppy diskette which maxed out at 1.44 MB (Megabytes) in capacity.

As I soon learned, hard disk drives and floppy disk drives did not possess the digital immortality I so confidently believed in. Sadly, many files, documents, and priceless fine art created in Microsoft Paint by yours truly were lost to the digital afterlife, never to be retrieved again. Sigh. The world shall never know.

It wasn't until years later that I came across an article on file recovery and associated tools while browsing the magical **World Wide Web** (**WWW**) on my lightning-fast 42 Kbps dial-up internet connection (made possible by my very expensive USRobotics dial-up modem), which sang the tune of the technology gods every time I'd try to connect to the realm of the internet. This process involved a stealthy ninja-like skill that would make even a black-ops team envious, as it involved doing so without my parents noticing, as this would prevent them from using the telephone line to make or receive phone calls. (Apologies dear Mother, Father, and older teenage sister).

The previous article on data recovery wasn't anywhere near as detailed and fact-filled as the many great peer-reviewed papers, journals, and books on digital forensics widely-available today. As a total novice (also referred to as a noob) in the field, I did learn a great deal about the basics of file systems, data and metadata, storage measurements, and the workings of various storage media.

It was at this time that, even though I had read about the Linux operating system and its various distributions (or distros), I began to get an understanding of why Linux distros were popular in data recovery and forensics.

At this time, I managed to bravely download the Auditor and Slax Linux distributions, again on a dial-up connection. Just downloading these operating systems was quite a feat, which left me feeling highly accomplished as I did not have any clue as to how to install them, let alone actually use them. In those days, easy-installation and GUIs were still under heavy development, as user friendly, or in my case, user unfriendly, as they were at the time (mostly due to my inexperience, lack of recommended hardware, and also lack of resources such as online forums, blogs, and YouTube...which I did not yet know about). I'll explain more about the Auditor and Slax operating systems in `Chapter 2`, *Installing Kali Linux*, including their role in the infamous BackTrack, and now Kali Linux, operating systems.

As time passed, I researched many tools found on various platforms for Windows, Macintosh, and many Linux distributions. I found that many of the tools used in digital forensics could be installed in various Linux distributions or flavors and many of these tools were well maintained, constantly being developed and were widely accepted by peers in the field. Kali Linux is a Linux distribution or flavor, but before we go any further, let me explain the concept of Linux distribution or flavor. Consider your favorite beverage: this beverage can come in many flavors, some without sweeteners or sugar, in different colors, and even in various sizes. No matter what the variations, it's still the basic ingredients that comprise the beverage, at the core. In this way, too, we have Linux, and then different types and varieties of Linux. Some more popular Linux distros and flavors include RedHat, CentOS, Ubuntu, Mint, Knoppix, and, of course, Kali Linux. More on Kali Linux will be discussed in `Chapter 2`, *Installing Kali Linux*.

For this book, we take a very structured approach to digital forensics, as we would in forensic science. We first stroll into the world of digital forensics, its history, some of the tools and operating systems used for forensics, and immediately introduce you to the concepts involved in evidence preservation.

How about we kick things off. Let's get started!

This chapter gives an introduction to the various aspects of the science of digital forensics.

The topics we are going to cover in this chapter are:

- What is digital forensics?
- Digital forensics methodology.
- A brief history of digital forensics.

- The need for digital forensics as technology advances.
- Anti-forensics: threats to digital forensics
- Commercial tools available in the field of digital forensics.
- Open source tools.
- Operating systems with built-in tools for digital forensics.
- The need for using multiple forensics tools in investigations in an effort to provide strong proof of integrity.

What is digital forensics?

The first thing I'd like to cover in this chapter is an understanding of digital forensics and its proper practices and procedures. At some point, you may have come across several books, blogs, and even videos demonstrating various aspects of digital forensics and different tools used. It is of great importance to understand that forensics itself is a science, involving very well documented best practices and methods in an effort to reveal whether something exists or does not.

Digital forensics involves the preservation, acquisition, documentation, analysis, and interpretation of evidence from various storage media types found. It is not only limited to laptops, desktops, tablets, and mobile devices, but also extends to data in transit which is transmitted across public or private networks.

In most cases, digital forensics involves the discovery and/or recovery of data using various methods and tools available to the investigator. Digital forensics investigations include, but are not limited to:

- **Data recovery**: Investigating and recovering data that may have been deleted, changed to different file extensions, and even hidden.
- **Identity theft**: Many fraudulent activities ranging from stolen credit card usage to fake social media profiles usually involve some sort of identity theft.
- **Malware and ransomware investigations**: To date, ransomware spread by Trojans and worms across networks and the internet are some of the biggest threats to companies, military organizations, and individuals. Malware can also be spread to and by mobile devices and smart devices.
- **Network and internet investigations**: Investigating **DoS** (known as **Denial-of-Service**) and **DDoS** (known as **Distributed DoS**) attacks and tracking down accessed devices including printers and files.

- **Email investigations**: Investigating the source and IP origins, attached content, and geo-location information can all be investigated.
- **Corporate espionage**: Many companies are moving away from print copies and toward cloud and traditional disk media. As such, a digital footprint is always left behind; should sensitive information be accessed or transmitted?
- **Child pornography investigations**: Sadly, the reality is that children are widely exploited on the internet and within the Deep Web. With the use of technology and highly-skilled forensic analysts, investigations can be carried out in bringing down exploitation rings by analyzing internet traffic, browser history, payment transactions, email records, and images.

Digital forensics methodology

Keeping in mind that forensics is a science, digital forensics requires that one follow appropriate best practices and procedures in an effort to produce the same results time and time again providing proof of evidence, preservation, and integrity which can be replicated ;if called upon to do so.

Although many people may not be performing digital forensics to be used as evidence in a court of law, it is best to practice in such a way as can be accepted and presented in a court of law. The main purpose of adhering to best-practices set by organizations specializing in digital forensics and incident response is to maintain the integrity of the evidence for the duration of the investigation. In the event that the investigator's work must be scrutinized and critiqued by another or an opposing party, the results found by the investigator must be able to be recreated, thereby proving the integrity of the investigation. The purpose of this is to ensure that your methods can be repeated and, if dissected or scrutinized, produce the same results time and again. The methodology used, including the procedures and findings of your investigation, should always allow for the maintenance of the data's integrity, regardless of what tools are used.

The best practices demonstrated in this book, ensure that the original evidence is not tampered with, or in cases of investigating devices and data in a live or production environment, show well-documented proof that necessary steps were taken during the investigation to avoid unnecessary tampering of the evidence, thereby preserving the integrity of the evidence. For those completely new to investigations, I recommend familiarizing yourself with some of the various practices and methodologies available and widely practiced by the professional community.

As such, there exist several guidelines and methodologies that one should adopt, or at least follow, to ensure that examinations and investigations are forensically sound.

The 2 best-practices documents mentioned in this chapter are:

- the ACPO's Good Practice Guide for Digital Evidence
- the SWGDE's Best Practices for Computer Forensics.

Although written in 2012, the **Association of Chief Police Officers**, known as the ACPO, and now functioning as the **National Police Chiefs' Council**, or NPCO, put forth a document in a PDF file called The *ACPO Good Practice Guide for Digital Evidence* in best practices when carrying out digital forensics investigations, particularly focusing on evidence acquisition. The *ACPO Good Practice Guide for Digital Evidence* was then adopted and adhered to by Law Enforcement agencies in England, Wales, and Northern Ireland and can be downloaded in its entirety at https://www.7safe.com/docs/default-source/default-document-library/acpo_guidelines_computer_evidence_v4_web.pdf.

Another useful and more recent document, produced in September 2014, on best practices in digital forensics was issued by the **Scientific Working Group on Digital Evidence (SWGDE)**. The SWGDE was founded in 1998 by the Federal Crime Laboratory Directors Group with major members and contributors including the FBI, DEA, NASA, and the Department of Defense Computer Forensics Laboratory. Though this document details procedures and practices within a formal computer forensics laboratory setting, the practices can still be applied to non-laboratory investigations by those not currently in or with access to such an environment.

The *SWGDE Best Practices for Computer Forensics* sheds light on many of the topics covered in the following chapters, including:

- Evidence collection and acquisition
- Investigating devices that are powered on and powered off
- Evidence handling
- Analysis and reporting

 The full document is publicly available at https://www.swgde.org/documents/Current%20Documents/SWGDE%20Best%20Practices%20for%20Computer%20Forensics.

A brief history of digital forensics

Although forensic science itself (including the first recorded fingerprints) has been around for over 100 years, digital forensics is a much younger field as it relates to the digital world, which mainly gained popularity after the introduction of personal computers in the 1980s.

For comparative purposes in trying to grasp the concept of digital forensics as still being relatively new, consider that the first actual forensic sciences lab was developed by the FBI in 1932.

Some of the first tools used in digital forensic investigations were developed in FBI labs circa 1984, with forensic investigations being spearheaded by the FBI's specialized **CART** (**Computer Analysis and Response Team**) which was responsible for aiding in digital investigations.

Digital forensics as its own field grew substantially in the 1990s, with the collaboration of several law enforcement agencies and heads of divisions working together and even meeting regularly to bring their expertise to the table.

One of the earliest formal conferences was hosted by the FBI in 1993. The main focus of the event, called the **International Law Enforcement Conference on Computer Evidence**, was to address the need for formal standards and procedures with digital forensics and evidence acquisition.

Many of these conferences resulted in the formation of bodies that deal with digital forensics standards and best practices. For example, the SWGDE was formed by the **Federal Crime Laboratory Directors** in 1998. The SWGDE was responsible for producing the widely adopted best practices for computer evidence (discussed later in this chapter). The SWGDE also collaborated with other organizations, such as the very popular **American Society of Crime Laboratory Directors** (**ASCLDs**), which was formed in 1973 and has since been instrumental in the ongoing development of best practices, procedures, and training as it relates to forensic science.

It wasn't until the early 2000s, however, that a formal **Regional Computer Forensic Laboratory** (**RCFL**) was established by the FBI. In 2002, the **National Program Office** (**NPO**) was established and acts as a central body, essentially coordinating and supporting efforts between RCFL's law enforcement.

Since then, we've seen several agencies, such as the FBI, CIA, NSA, and GCHQ, each with their own full cyber crime divisions, full digital forensics labs, dedicated onsite and field agents, collaborating assiduously in an effort to take on tasks that may be nothing short of **Sisyphean**, when considering the rapid growth of technology and easier access to the internet and even the Dark Web.

With the advancement of technology, the tools for digital forensics must be regularly updated, not only in the fight against cyber crime, but in the ability to provide accountability and for the retrieval of lost data. We've come a long way since the days of floppy disks, magnetic drives, and dial-up internet access, and are now presented with SD cards, solid-state drives, and fiber-optic internet connections at Gigabit speeds.

The need for digital forensics as technology advances

Some of you may be young-at-heart enough to remember the days of Windows 95, 3.x, and even **DOS (Disk Operating System)**. Smart watches, calculators, and many IoT devices today are much faster than the first generation of personal computers and servers. In 1995, it was common to come across hard disk drives between 4 GB to 10 GB, whereas today you can easily purchase drives with capacities of 2 TB and up.

Consider also the various types of storage media today, including Flash drives, SD cards, CDs, DVDs, Blu-ray discs, hybrid and solid-state drives, as compared to the older floppy disks, which at their most compact and efficient only stored 1.44 MB of data on a 3 ¼ inch disk. Although discussed in detail in a later chapter, we now have many options for not only storing data but also losing and hiding data.

With the advancement of technology also comes a deeper understanding of programming languages, operating systems both average and advanced, and knowledge and utilization of digital devices. This also translates into more user-friendly interfaces which can accomplish many of the same tasks as with the CLI, used mainly by advanced users. Essentially, today's simple GUI, together with a wealth of resources readily found on search engines, can make certain tasks, such as hiding data, far easier than before.

Hiding large amounts of data is also simpler today, considering the speed of processors, combined with large amounts of RAM, including devices which can also act as RAM, far surpass those of as recent as five years ago. Graphics cards must also be mentioned and taken into consideration, as more and more mobile devices are being outfitted with very powerful high-end onboard NVIDIA and ATI cards which also have their own separate RAM, aiding the process. Considering all these factors does lend support to the idea put forth by Gordon E. Moore in the 1970s that states that computing power doubles every two years, commonly known as Moore's Law.

However, Jensen Huang, CEO of NVIDIA, has recently stated that Moore's Law is dying as GPUs (Graphic Processing Units) will ultimately replace CPUs due to the GPU's performance, technological advancements and abilities in handling artificial intelligence. Huang's statement was also mirrored by Intel CEO Brian Krzanich.

All things considered, several avenues for carrying out cyber crimes are now available, including malware and ransomware distribution, DoS and DDoS attacks, espionage, blackmail, identity theft, data theft, illegal online activities and transactions and a plethora of other malicious activities. Many of these activities are anonymous as they occur over the internet and often take place using masked IP addresses and public networks and so, make investigations that much harder for the relevant agencies in pinpointing locations and apprehending suspects.

With cyber crime being such a big business, the response from law enforcement officials and agencies must be equally impressive in their research, development, intelligence, and training divisions if they are to put up a fight in what may seem like a never-ending battle in the digital world.

Digital forensics not only applies to storage media but also to network and internet connections, mobile devices, IoT devices, and in reality, any device that can store, access, or transmit data. As such, we have a variety of tools, both commercial and open source, available to us depending on the task at hand.

Commercial tools available in the field of digital forensics

Although this book focuses on tools within the Kali Linux operating system, it's important to recognize the commercially-available tools available to us, many of which you can download as trial or demo versions before determining a preference.

Because this book focuses primarily on open source tools, I'll just make mention of some of the more popular commercial tools available along with their homepages. The tools are listed only in alphabetical order and do not reflect any ratings, reviews, or the author's personal preference:

- EnCase® Forensic: `https://www.guidancesoftware.com/encase-forensic`
- F-Response: `https://www.f-response.com/`
- Forensic Toolkit: `http://accessdata.com/products-services/forensic-toolkit-ftk`
- Helix Enterprise: `http://www.e-fense.com/h3-enterprise.php`
- Magnet Axiom: `https://www.magnetforensics.com/computer-forensics/`
- X-Ways Forensics: `http://www.x-ways.net/forensics/index-m.html`

Many of the commercial tools available all allow for the following features and also offer several proprietary features, including:

- Write blocking
- Bit-by-bit or bit-stream copies and disk cloning/evidence cloning
- Forensically sound evidence acquisition
- Evidence preservation using hashes
- File recovery (hidden and deleted)
- Live and remote acquisition of evidence
- RAM and swap/paging file analysis
- Image mounting (supporting various formats)
- Advanced data and metadata (data about data) searches and filtering
- Bookmarking of files and sectors
- Hash and password cracking
- Automatic report generation

The main advantage of commercial tools is that they are usually automated and are actually a suite of tools that can almost always perform entire investigations, from start to finish, with a few clicks. Another advantage that I must mention is the support for the tools that are given with the purchase of a license. The developers of these tools also employ research and development teams to ensure constant testing and review of their current and new products.

Operating systems and open source tools for digital forensics

Just as there are several commercial tools available, there exist many open source tools available to investigators, amateur and professional alike. Many of these tools are Linux-based and can be found on several freely-available forensic distributions.

The main question that usually arises when choosing tools is usually based on commercial versus open source. Whether using commercial tools or open source tools, the end result should be the same, with preservation and integrity of the original evidence being the main priority.

 Budget is always an issue and some commercial tools (as robust, accurate, and user-friendly as they might be) can cost thousands of dollars.

The open source tools are free to use under various open source licenses and should not be counted out just because they are not backed by enterprise developers and researchers. Many of the open source tools are widely reviewed by the forensic community and may be open to more scrutiny, as they are more widely available to the public and are built in non-proprietary code.

Though the focus of this book is on the forensic tools found in Kali Linux, which we will begin looking at toward the end of this section and onward, here are some of the more popular open source forensic distributions, or distros, available.

Each of the distros mentioned in the following sections is freely available at many locations but, for security reasons, we will provide the direct link from their homepages. The operating systems featured in this section are listed only in alphabetical order and do not reflect any ratings, reviews, or even the author's personal preference.

Digital evidence and forensics toolkit Linux

Digital Evidence and Forensics Toolkit (DEFT) Linux comes in a full version and a lighter version called **DEFT Zero**. For forensic purposes, you may wish to download the full version as the Zero version, does not support mobile forensics and password-cracking features.

- **Homepage**: http://www.deftlinux.net/about/
- **Based on**: Ubuntu Desktop
- **Distribution type**: Forensics and incident response

Like the other distros mentioned in this list, DEFT, as shown in the following screenshot, is also a fully capable **live response** forensic tool that can be used on the go in situations where shutting down the machine is not possible and also allows for on-the-fly analysis of RAM and the swap file:

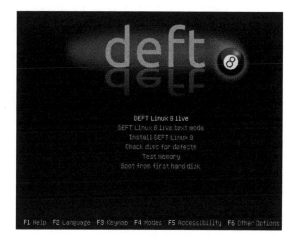

When booting from the DEFT Linux DVD, bootable flash, or other media, the user is presented with various options, including the options to install DEFT Linux to the hard disk, or use as a live-response tool or operating system by selecting the **DEFT Linux 8 live** option, as shown here:

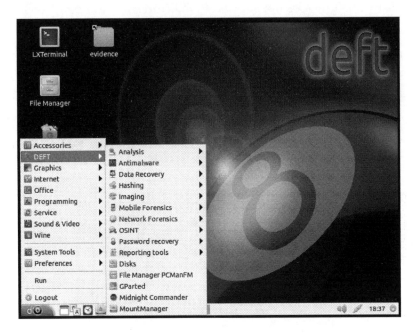

In the previous screenshot, it can be seen that there are several forensic categories in DEFT Linux 8 such as **Antimalware, Data Recovery, Hashing, Imaging, Mobile Forensics**, and **Network Forensics, Password recovery**, and **Reporting tools**. Within each category exist several tools created by various developers, giving the investigator quite a variety from which to choose.

For a full list of the features and packages included in the **Digital Evidence Forensic Toolkit (DEFT)** Linux OS at the time of this publishing, please visit the following link:

```
http://www.deftlinux.net/package-list/
```

Computer Aided INvestigative Environment

The **Computer Aided INvestigative Environment (CAINE)** is a live-response bootable CD/DVD with options for booting in safe mode, text mode, as a live system, or in RAM, as shown here:

- **Homepage**: http://www.caine-live.net/
- **Based on**: GNU Linux.
- **Distribution type**: Forensics and incident response

One of the most noticeable features of CAINE after selecting your boot option is the easy way to find the write-blocker feature, seen and labeled as a **BlockON/OFF** icon, as shown in the following screenshot. Activating this feature prevents the writing of data by the CAINE OS to the evidence machine or drive:

Forensic Tools is the first menu listed in CAINE. Like DEFT Linux, there are several categories in the menu, as seen in the following screenshot, with several of the more popular tools used in open source forensics. Besides the categories, there are direct links to some of the more well-known tools, such as **Guymager** and **Autopsy**, which will both be covered in detail in later chapters:

For a full list of the features and packages included in CAINE at the time of this publishing, please visit the following link:

```
http://www.caine-live.net/page11/page11.html
```

Kali Linux

Finally, we get to this lovely gem, Kali Linux, fully discussed in detail from its installation to advanced forensics usage in the next chapter and throughout this book.

- **Homepage**: https://www.kali.org/
- **Based on**: Debian
- **Distribution type**: Penetration testing, forensics, and anti-forensics

Kali Linux was created as a penetration testing or pen-testing distro under the name BackTrack, which then evolved into Kali Linux, in 2015. This powerful tool is the definite tool of choice for penetration testers and security enthusiasts worldwide. As a **Certified EC-Council Instructor (CEI)** for the **Certified Ethical Hacker (CEH)** course, this operating system is usually the star of the class due to its many impressive bundled security programs, ranging from scanning and reconnaissance tools to advanced exploitation tools and reporting tools.

Like the above-mentioned tools, Kali Linux can be used as a live response forensic tool, as it contains many of the tools required for full investigations. Kali, however, can also be used as a complete operating system, as it can be fully installed to a hard disk or flash drive and also contains several tools for productivity and entertainment. It comes with many of the required drivers for successful use of hardware, graphics, and networking, and also runs smoothly on both 32 bit and 64 bit systems with minimal resources; it can also be installed on certain mobile devices, such as **Nexus** and **OnePlus** phones and tablets.

Adding to its versatility, upon booting from a live CD/DVD or flash drive, the investigator has several options to choose from, including **Live (forensic mode)**, which leaves the evidence drive intact and does not tamper with it by also disabling any auto-mounting of flash drives and other storage media, providing for integrity of the original evidence throughout the investigation.

When booting to Kali Linux from a DVD or flash drive, the user is first presented with options for a live environment and installation. Choosing the third option from the list carries us into **Live (forensic mode)**, as seen in the following screenshot:

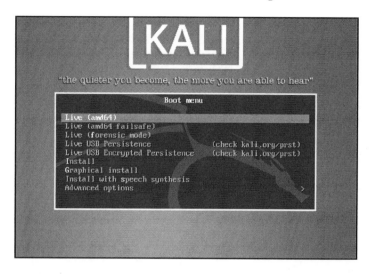

Once Kali **Live (forensic mode)** has booted, the investigator is presented with the exact same home screen as would be seen if using any of the GUIs in Kali, as shown in the following screenshot:

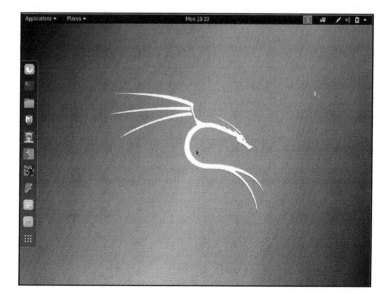

The Kali menu can be found at the top left corner by clicking on **Applications**. This brings the user to the menu listing which shows the forensics category lower down, as **11 - Forensics**. The following screenshot gives an idea of some of the **Forensic** tools available in Kali that we'll be using later on in the book:

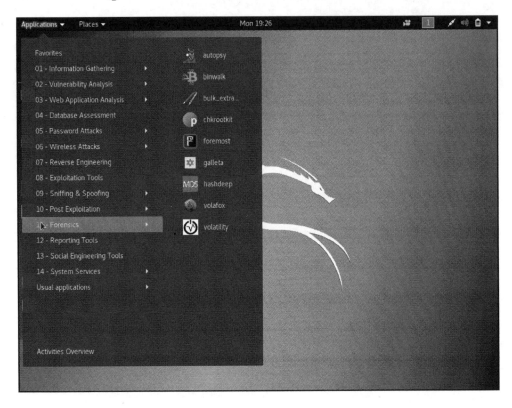

It should be noted that the tools listed are not the only tools available in Kali. There are several other tools that can be brought up via the Terminal, as we'll see in later chapters.

It's also noteworthy that, when it is in forensic mode, not only does Kali not tamper with the original evidence drive but also does not write data to the swap file, where important data that was recently accessed and stored in memory may reside.

The following screenshot shows another view of accessing the **Forensic** tools menu using the last icon in the list on the sidebar menu (resembling nine dots in a square formation):

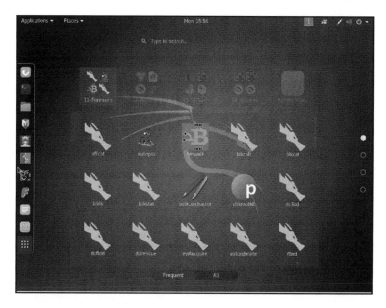

For a full list of the features and packages included in the Kali Linux operating system at the time of this publishing, please visit the following link:

https://tools.kali.org/tools-listing

Out of the three forensic distros mentioned, Kali can operate as a live response forensic tool, but can also be used as a full operating system, just like Windows, Mac, and Android as it contains several built-in tools for productivity and everyday use. The fact that Kali can be installed to a hard disk means that several other tools can be downloaded and updated regularly, giving continuous access to all IT security and forensic tools, allowing the user to save progress as they use the tools and not have to worry too much about restarting their machine should they decide to use it as a full operating system.

Using these open source forensic operating systems, such as Kali, gives us a range of tools to choose from and work with. There exist many tools for performing the same tasks within each category in the distros. This is good, because our findings should be able to be replicated using different tools. This is especially good in instances where the investigator's work may be critiqued and the integrity of the case and evidence questioned and scrutinized; using multiple tools correctly will yield consistent results.

The need for multiple forensics tools in digital investigations

Preservation of evidence is of the utmost importance. Using commercial and open source tools correctly will yield results; however, for forensically sound results, it is sometimes best if more than one tool can be used and produce the same results.

Another reason to use multiple tools may simply be cost. Some of us may have a large budget to work with, while others may have a limited one or none at all. Commercial tools can be costly, especially due to research and development, testing, advertising, and other factors. Open source tools, while tested by the community, may not have the available resources and funding as with commercial tools.

So then, how do we know which tools to choose?

Digital forensics is often quite time-consuming, which is one of the reasons you may wish to work with multiple forensic copies of the evidence. This way you can use different tools simultaneously in an effort to speed up the investigation. While fast tools may be a good thing, we should also question the reliability and accuracy of the tools.

The **National Institute of Standards and Technology (NIST)** has developed a **Computer Forensics Tool Testing (CFTT)** program that tests digital forensic tools and makes all findings available to the public. Several tools are chosen based on their specific abilities and placed into testing categories such as disk imaging, carving, and file recovery. Each category has a formal test plan and strategy for testing along with a validation report, again available to the public.

More on the CFTT program can be found at `https://www.cftt.nist.gov/disk_imaging.htm`. Testing and validation reports on many of the tools covered in this book can be found at `https://www.dhs.gov/science-and-technology/nist-cftt-reports`.

To re-enforce the importance of using multiple tools in maintaining the integrity of your investigations and findings, multiple tools will be demonstrated in the third and fourth sections of this book.

Anti-forensics: threats to digital forensics

As much as we would like the tasks involved in digital forensics to be as easy as possible, we do encounter situations which make investigations, and life as a forensics investigator, not-so-simple and sometimes stressful. People wishing to hide information, cover their tracks, and even those who have malicious intent or actually participate in cyber crimes often employ various methods to try to foil the attempts of forensic investigators with the hope of hampering or halting investigations.

Within somewhat recent times we've seen several major digital breaches online, especially from 2011 onward. Many of these attacks allegedly came from, or were claimed to be the work of, infamous hacker groups such as LulzSec, Anonymous, Lizard Squad, and many others, including individuals and Hacktivists (people that hack for a specific cause or reason and are less concerned about doing time in prison). Some of these hacks and attacks not only brought down several major networks and agencies, but also cost millions in damage, directly and indirectly; as a result, the loss of public confidence in the companies contributed to further increases in damages.

These daring, creative, and public attacks saw the emergence of many other new groups that learned from the mistakes of past breaches of Anonymous and others. Both social media and underground communication channels soon became the easiest forms of communication between like-minded hackers and hacktivists. With the internet and World Wide Web becoming easily accessible, this also saw the competition not only between IPs, but also private companies and corporations, which lead to the creation of free wireless hotspots on almost every street with businesses, small or large.

The result of having internet access at just about every coffee shop enabled anyone with a smartphone, tablet, laptop, or other devices to acquire almost unauthenticated access to the internet. This gave them access to hacker sites and portals, along with the ability to download tools, upload malware, send infected emails, or even carry out attacks.

Encryption

Adding to this scenario is the availability of more user-friendly tools to aid in the masking of **Publicly Identifiable Information (PII)**, or any information that would aid in the discovery of unveiling suspects involved in cyber-crimes during forensic investigations. Tools used for encryption of data and anonymity, such as masking of IP addresses, are readily and easily available to anyone, most of which were and are increasingly more and more user-friendly.

It should also be noted that many Wi-Fi hotspots themselves can be quite dangerous, as these can be easily set up to intercept personal data, such as login and password information together with PII (such as social security numbers, date of birth info, and phone numbers) from any user that may connect to the Wi-Fi and enter such information.

The process of encryption provides confidentiality between communication parties and uses technology in very much the same way we use locks and keys to safeguard our personal and private belongings. For a lock to open, there must be a specific matching key. So too, in the digital world, data is encrypted or locked using an encryption algorithm and must use either the same key to decrypt or unlock the data. There also exists another scenario where one key may be used to encrypt or lock the data and another used to decrypt the data. Two such very popular encryption tools are TrueCrypt and VeraCrypt.

These two encryption tools use very high encryption methods that keep data very confidential. The main barrier to forensics may be acquiring the decryption key to decrypt or unlock access to the data.

 TrueCrypt and VeraCrypt not only encrypt files but also encrypt folders, partitions, and entire drives!

Online and offline anonymity

Encryption, in particular, can make investigations rather difficult, but there is also the concept of anonymity which adds to the complexity of maintaining an accuracy of the true sources found in investigations. Like encryption, there exist several free and open source tools for all operating system platforms, such as Windows, Mac, Linux, and Android, which attempt and most often successfully mask the hiding of someone's digital footprint. This digital footprint usually identifies a device by its IP address and **MAC (Media Access Control)** address. Without going into the network aspect of things, these two digital addresses can be compared to a person's full name and home address, respectively.

Even though a person's IP address can change according to their private network (home and work) and public network (internet) access, the MAC address remains the same. However, various tools are also freely available to spoof or fake one's IP and MAC addresses for the purpose of privacy and anonymity. Adding to that, users can use a system of routing their data through online servers and devices to make the tracing of the source of the sent data quite difficult. This system is referred to as proxy chaining and does keep some of the user's identity hidden.

A good example of this would be the Tor browser; it uses onion routing and several proxies worldwide to route or passes the data along from proxy to proxy, making the tracing of the source very difficult, but not impossible. You can think of proxy chains as a relay race, but instead of having four people, one passing the baton to the next, the data is passed between hundreds of proxy devices, worldwide.

Summary

Congratulations! You made it to the end of the first chapter. Before we jump into the second chapter, let's have a look at what was just covered.

We saw that digital forensics is still a relatively new field, although forensic science has been around for a very long time, as far back as the early 1900s. Although digital forensics may have only been on the scene since the early 2000s, as a science, we have certain best practices, procedures, and standards, such as those created by the ACPO and SWGDE, to adhere to. These maintain accuracy and the integrity of both the findings and the actual evidence when carrying out investigations, whether as an amateur or professional Digital Forensic Investigator.

Some of the commercial tools mentioned were EnCase, FTK, and Magnet Forensics. Many of the open source tools available are made for Linux-based distributions and can be downloaded individually, but many are readily and easily available within certain Forensic and Security Operating Systems or distributions. Some of these distros are DEFT Linux, CAINE, and of course, Kali Linux; all of these are freely available for download at the links provided.

I hope this introduction to digital forensics was informative and fun for you. Now that we've gotten a foundation of forensics, let's go deeper into Kali Linux as we learn how to download, install and update Kali in `Chapter 2`, *Installing Kali Linux*. See you on the next page.

2
Installing Kali Linux

Here we are. Join me as we get started by installing Kali Linux. Some of our readers may already be familiar with the installation process, and perhaps even some of the advanced features such as partitioning and networking. For the beginners and those new to Kali Linux, we encourage you to pay particular attention to this chapter, as we begin from the absolute basics of downloading Kali Linux, working our way up to a successful installation.

The topics that we are going to cover in this chapter are:

- Software version
- Downloading Kali Linux
- Installing Kali Linux
- Installing Kali Linux in VirtualBox

Software version

Kali has been around for quite some time. Known previously as BackTrack, with releases from versions one to five, Kali Linux was first seen in 2015 and released as Kali 1.0. From 2016 onward, Kali was then named according to the year. For instance, at the time of writing this book, the version used was Kali 2017.2, released in September 2017.

For those running older versions of Kali, or purchasing this book at a later date where new versions of Kali Linux may be available, you can easily update your instance of Kali Linux by using the `sudo apt-get update distro` command, demonstrated toward the end of this chapter.

Downloading Kali Linux

For safety and security reasons, it is always best to download Kali Linux directly from the website of its creators, **Offensive Security**. The main reason for this being that the downloads of Kali on other pages could possibly be fake, or worse, infected with malware such as Trojans, rootkits, and even ransomware. Offensive Security has also included hashes of all versions of Kali downloads on their site, allowing users to compare the hash of their downloaded version of Kali with what was generated and posted by Offensive Security on their website (`https://www.kali.org`). Once there, you can click on the **Downloads** link ,or go directly to the Kali Linux **Downloads** page by visiting `https://www.kali.org/downloads/`.

Once on the **Downloads** page, we can see six download versions of Kali available for download, each with specific category information:

- **Image Name**: Specifies the name of the download as well as whether the operating system is 32-bit or 64-bit.

32-bit operating systems are limited to utilizing only 4 GB of RAM. Should you have a system with more than 4 GB of RAM, you may wish to download the 64-bit version of Kali Linux.

- **Download**: ISO (an acronym for **International Standard Organization**) downloads directly via the user's browser. Torrent requires special software to be installed in order to be downloaded.

ISO files (or ISO images, as they are commonly called) are exact copies of data used specifically when duplicating data.

- **Size**: File size in GB.
- **Version**: Version of Kali Linux.

- **sha256sum**: Command used in Linux to generate a checksum or digital output representing the existing data, which can then be used to compare against the checksum of the downloaded copy to ensure that no data or bits were changed or tampered with:

Blog   Downloads   Training   Documen

Kali Linux Downloads

Download Kali Linux Images

We generate fresh Kali Linux image files every few months, which we make available for download. This page provides the links to **download Kali Linux** in its latest official release. For a release history, check our Kali Linux Releases page. Please note: You can find unofficial, untested weekly releases at http://cdimage.kali.org/kali-weekly/.

Image Name	Download	Size	Version	sha256sum
Kali 64 bit	ISO | Torrent	2.8G	2017.2	4556775bfb981ae64a3cb19aa0b73e8dcac6e4ba524f31c4bc14c9137b99725d
Kali 32 bit	ISO | Torrent	2.9G	2017.2	7f5000d8f55469264399a8bb7358fc22bec87fb1dc8a51b87f26876634e3effc
Kali 64 bit Light	ISO	0.8G	2017.2	369a29deff40dfff4f53fb47a6015d41d4ada8833a0b6e159657d2f223670f8b
Kali 32 bit Light	ISO	0.8G	2017.2	f6ee21b2880501caee8aa47960e8f424dab5fae1a13ba4b4e02d45152b6acd0d
Kali 64 bit e17	ISO | Torrent	2.6G	2017.2	20dee81d9891aa6dcfe505a68692f98f981b43a14234d18d9edd92373d6ed6ab
Kali 64 bit Mate	ISO | Torrent	2.8G	2017.2	9c99a2cc52b1d48875681d12e1fcf6b0b003d44f7ceb610438b5bea148414810

For this book, we'll be using the Kali 64-bit, downloaded as an ISO image as seen here:

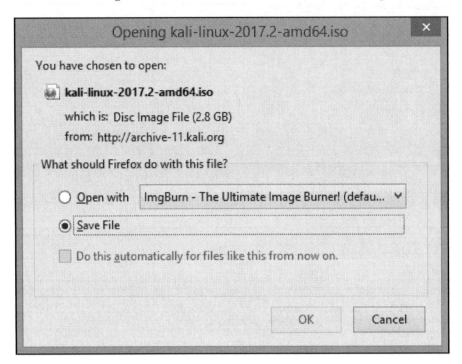

Installing Kali Linux

As mentioned in Chapter 1, *Introduction to Digital Forensics*, Kali Linux can be used as a live response operating system as well as a full operating system, installed and run from a hard disk. After downloading Kali Linux, the ISO image can be burnt to a DVD using any ISO file burning tool, such as ImgBurn. The DVD can then be used as a live OS, or it can also be used to install Kali to a hard disk. Tools such as UNetbootin can also be used to install Kali Linux to removable storage media, including a flash drive, SD card, or external hard disk drive, depending on the user's preference.

For use along with this book, I recommend that you first burn Kali Linux to a DVD and then install Kali onto a new hard drive, thereby catering to the concept of forensic readiness. In this instance, forensic readiness refers to the hard drive being brand new and untouched, therefore not compromised in any way, so as to maintain the integrity of both investigator and investigation.

For those who may not have the available resources to install Kali Linux on a brand new drive, there is also the option of installing Kali Linux within a virtual environment. Users can use virtualization technology such as VMware and VirtualBox to be able to run the Kali Linux OS as a guest machine within their host machine.

Installing Kali Linux in VirtualBox

VirtualBox can run on many platforms, including Windows, macOS, Linux, and Solaris. In this section, we install **VirtualBox 5.1.28** into our host machine and take it from there.

VirtualBox can be found at `https://www.virtualbox.org/wiki/Downloads`:

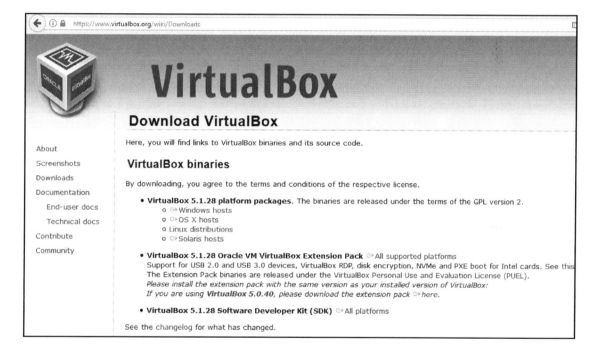

Preparing the Kali Linux virtual machine

Once VirtualBox has been downloaded, it can be installed and then configured to run Kali Linux and many other operating systems, depending on the amount of RAM available.

When setting up a new guest OS or guest virtual machine, we first click on **New** and then fill in the following details:

- **Name**: `Kali-Forensic` (or name of your choice)
- **Type: Linux**
- **Version: Debian (64-bit)**

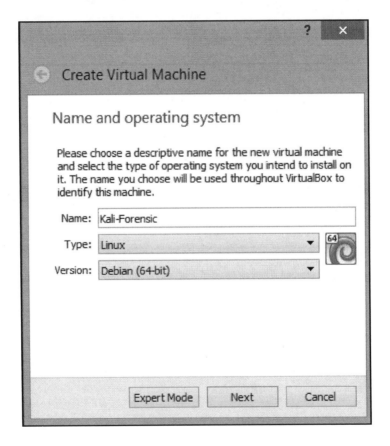

We then click **Next** and proceed to allocate RAM in the **Memory size** prompt:

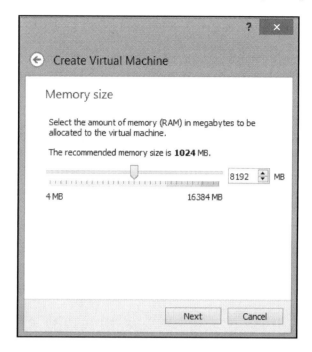

In the preceding **Memory size** screenshot, we can see the maximum RAM capacity to the right of the screen. The machine I used has 16,384 MB (rounded off to 16 GB) of RAM. Although the recommended memory size for Kali is a meager 1024 MB (1 GB), I do recommend at least 4 GB of RAM for smooth functionality when using the forensic tools. I have allocated 8,192 MB of RAM for use on my virtual machine.

Next, we create the virtual machine by adding a virtual hard disk. I recommend starting with a new virtual hard disk, which is the second option in the selection. Click on **Create** to proceed, and then choose **VDI (VirtualBox Disk Image)** as the **Hard disk file type**:

Select **VDI** and click **Next**:

Once VDI has been selected, choose the **Dynamically allocated** option to allow the virtual hard disk to be expanded, if the need arise:

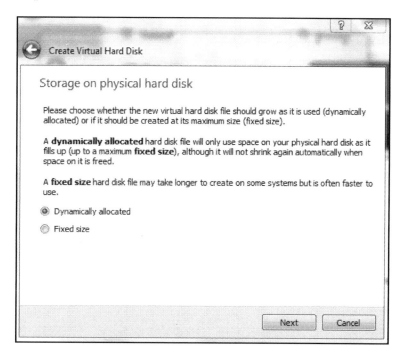

For the next step, we select the file location and the size of the virtual hard disk chosen. The recommended size for the Kali Linux VDI is 8 GB, but I assigned a generous 64 GB in the event that I may need to store copies of files and imaged drives on the Kali VM (virtual machine).

Once finished, click on **Create** to complete the creation of the virtual hard disk:

Installing Kali Linux on the virtual machine

Once the virtual hard disk has been prepared and completed by following the steps from the previous section, we can then begin the actual Kali Linux installation process. In the **Oracle VM VirtualBox Manager,** which is the main OS management window for VirtualBox, we can see that the VM prepared for our Kali Linux installation is now available.

To the middle of the screen, we can also see the resources assigned, such as the **Name** and **Operating System** type in the **General** section, and the amount of RAM assigned in the **System** section. Other settings, such as the **VRAM** (an acronym for **Video RAM**), **Network** and **Display** settings can also be accessed within this section.

To begin our Kali Linux installation, click on the **Kali-Forensic** entry to the left and click on the green start arrow:

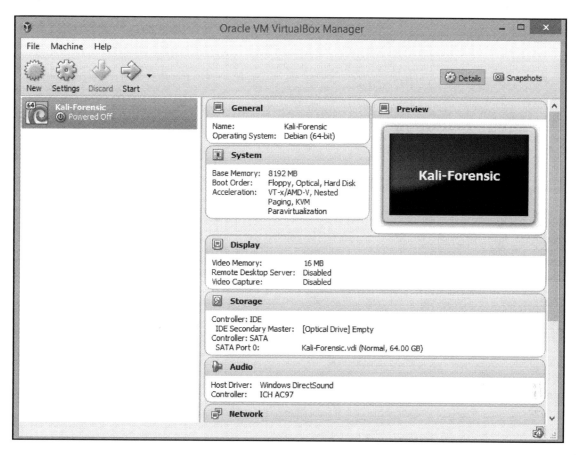

In the next step, we must locate the Kali Linux ISO image that we downloaded from the Offensive Security website. Click on the folder icon next to **Host Drive 'D:'** and search for the downloaded Kali Linux ISO image:

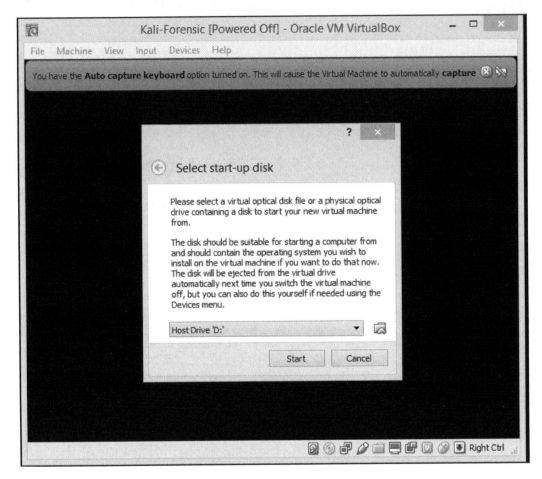

Once the ISO image is selected, you will notice the selected entry changes to **kali-linux-2017.2-amd64.iso (2.81 GB)**. Click on **Start** to begin the boot process:

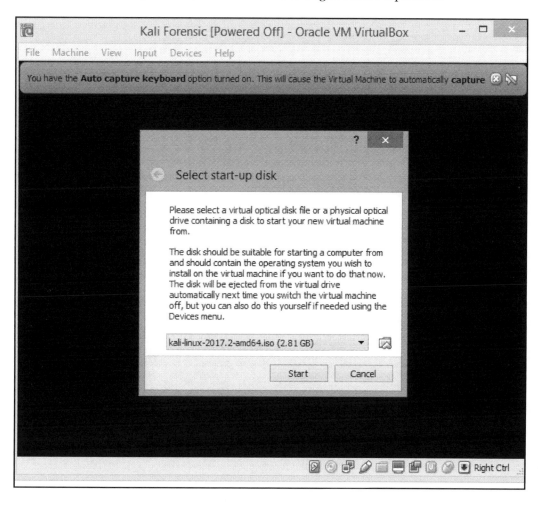

After clicking on **Start**, the **Boot menu** displays the various options available, including the live versions of Kali. For this demonstration, we'll be choosing the **Graphical install** option to install Kali to the virtual hard drive:

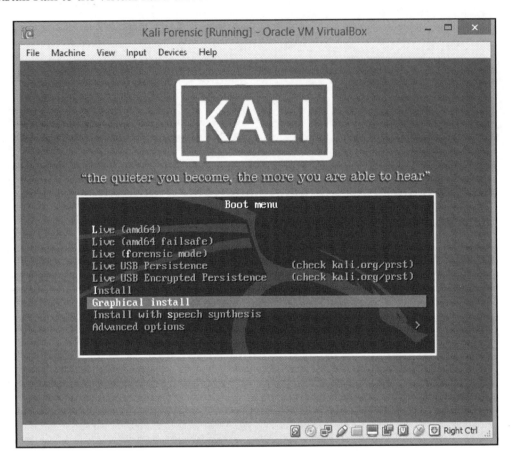

 As a side note, I should also draw your attention to the **Live (forensic mode)** option, which would be available to us when booting from a DVD, flash drive, or other removable storage media. It's a good idea to always have a copy of Kali Linux, in the event that a live response may be needed.

Ok, back to our installation. After clicking on the **Graphical install** option from the **Boot menu**, we're prompted to choose our language, location, and keyboard layout.

In the next step, we give our Kali Linux guest a **Hostname,** which is the same as a username in a Windows environment:

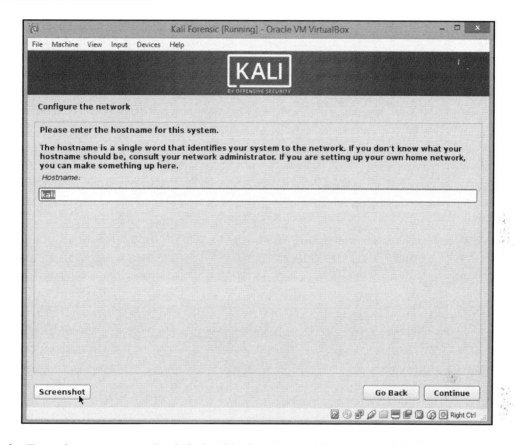

For the **Domain name** area, I've left this blank, as I won't be joining this host machine to a domain.

When setting the password, be sure to use one that you can remember. It makes no sense using a complex password, 16 characters long and consisting of uppercase and lowercase letters, and alphanumeric characters, if you can't remember the password upon booting:

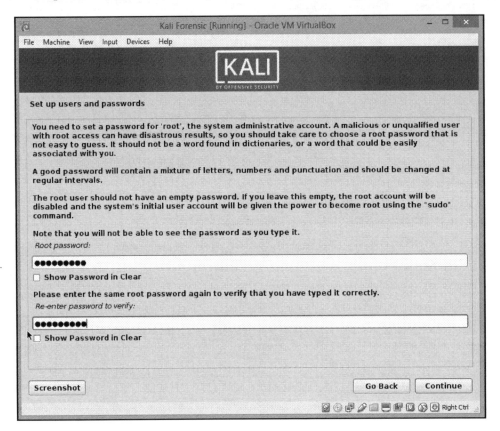

Partitioning the disk

Partition of the hard disk (whether virtual or physical) involves splitting the drive into logical drives. Think of it as having a large apartment studio comprising one large room. Now imagine that you've put up a wall to separate the apartment in half. It's still physically one apartment, but now it's separated into two rooms. One can be used as the main apartment and the other as storage, or you can even have two smaller apartments to share with yourself and a friend. Equally, a partition can allow for the installation of multiple operating systems on a hard disk, or even create additional volumes to use as storage space.

Continuing with our Kali Linux installation, the next step provides options on the usage of the virtual disk for partitioning. As this is a virtual disk, I recommend using the **Guided - use entire disk** partitioning method. This method is very simple, and uses all available allocated space assigned to the virtual disk in the preceding steps. Firstly, let's select the recommended partitioning method:

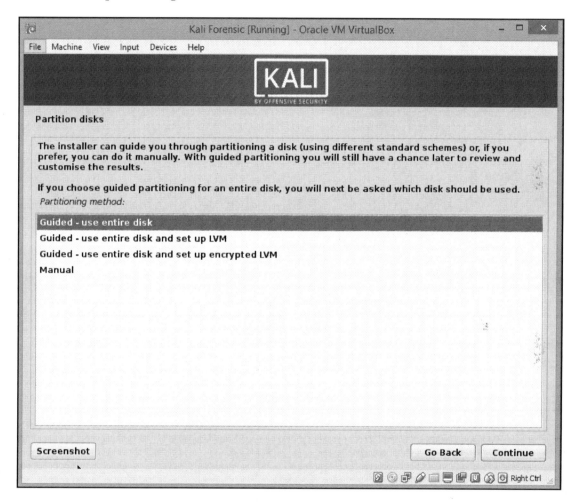

The other options in the screenshot above, present the user with options for setting up LVM (Logical Volume Manager) and encrypted LVM. The LVM manages logical partitions and can create, resize and delete Linux partitions.

The prompt warns that all data (if any) on the disk will be erased if choosing this option; however, this is a new virtual disk with no existing data on it, so we can continue with our installation.

After selecting the VirtualBox disk as seen in the following screenshot, be sure to select **All files in one partition**:

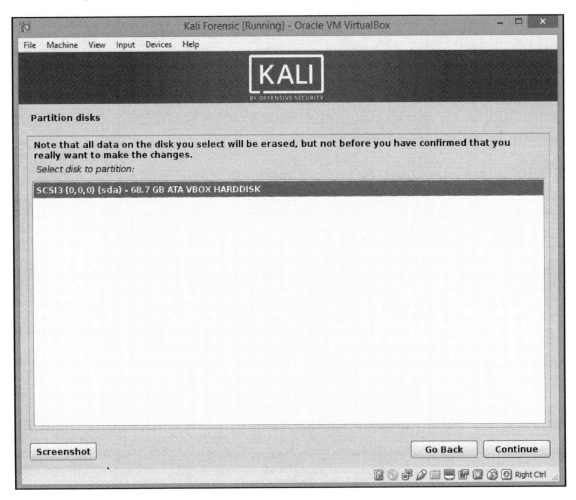

As we continue the partitioning process, one of the main reasons I've recommended the **guided partition** option is because it does almost everything for us. From here, we simply choose the last available option, which says **Finish partitioning and write changes to disk**, followed by clicking **Continue**:

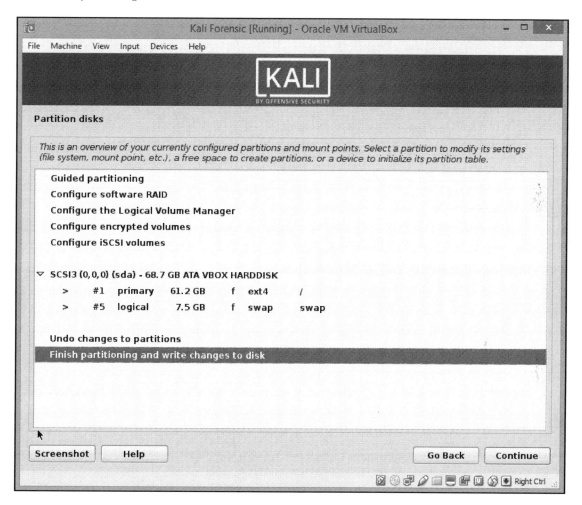

The last step in the partitioning process asks for confirmation to write the specified configurations and changes to the disk. Be sure to choose **Yes** before clicking on **Continue**:

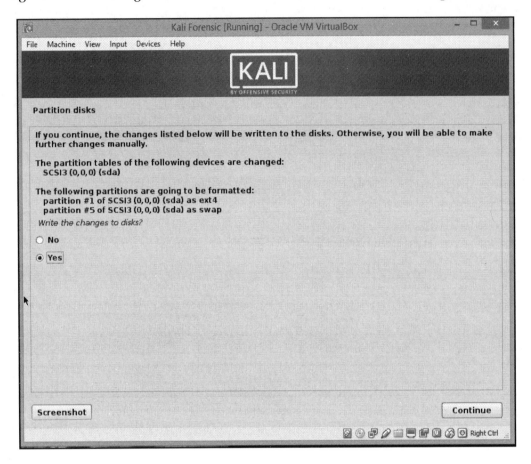

We're now just a few clicks away from having our Kali Linux VM installed and operational.

After the installation is complete, the **Package Manager** prompts to choose a network mirror, which allows us access to newer versions of the software. I'd advise skipping this step by clicking on **No**, as we will soon be installing our updates for Kali manually once we're up and running.

One of the last steps to take in the installation process is to **Install the GRUB boot loader on a hard disk**. Without going into too much detail, the **GRUB (GRand Unified Bootloader)** allows for a multiboot environment by allowing the user to safely have and choose between operating systems at boot screen, preserving the boot entries for each installed OS.

Although we can choose not to install GRUB (as we only have one OS installed on our virtual hard disk), the **Yes** option should be chosen if dual or multibooting with other OSes:

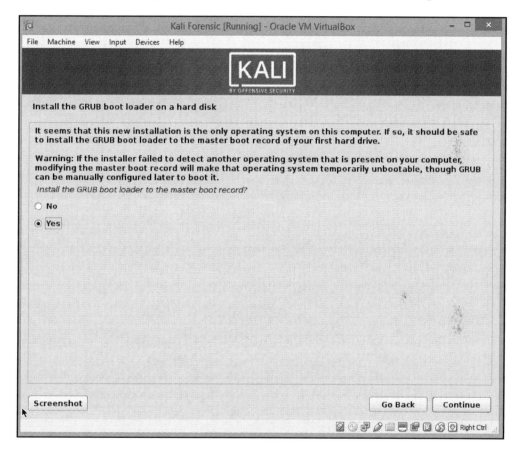

If choosing **Yes** to install GRUB, be sure to select the bootable device:

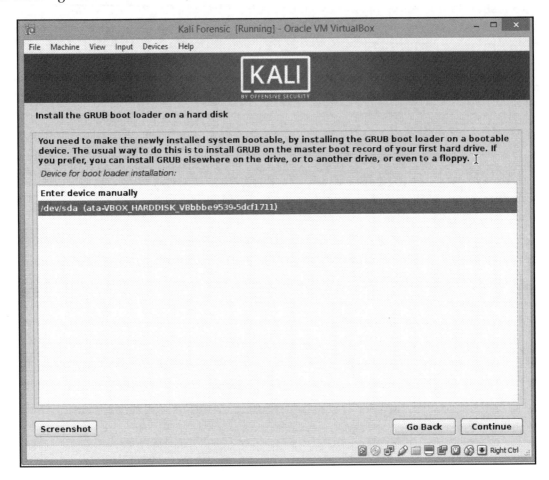

After clicking on **Continue**, the installation completes and boots into Kali Linux.

Exploring Kali Linux

Once our installation is complete, we can start Kali Linux. To log in, enter root as the **Username** and the password you previously configured:

When logged in, one of the first things we should do is enter three commands in the Terminal to update Kali.

To get to the Terminal (which is the equivalent of the Command Prompt in Windows), click on **Applications** | **Terminal**.

With the Terminal open, enter the following commands so that Kali can check for package updates, software upgrades, and distribution/distro updates:

- `apt-get update`
- `apt-get upgrade`
- `apt-get dist-update`

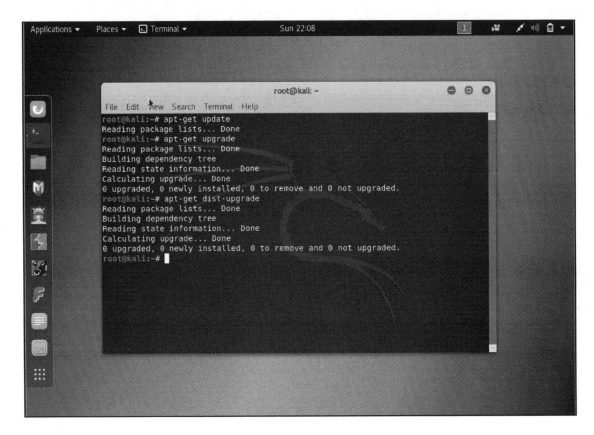

At this point, we have a successful updated installation of Kali Linux. As this book deals with digital forensics in Kali Linux, we can dive right in by taking a look at some of the tools for forensics available on the menu.

There are two ways to get to the **Forensics** menu in Kali Linux:

- The first is to click on **Applications,** and then move down to menu item number **11 - Forensics**, as seen in the following screenshot:

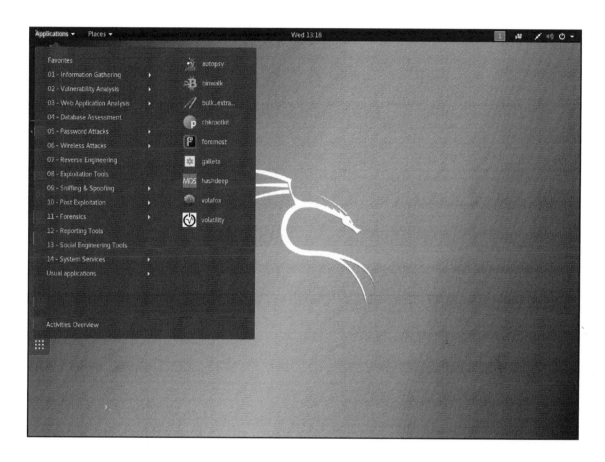

- For the second method, simply click on the **Show Applications** item (last icon in the floating side menu) and choose **Forensics**:

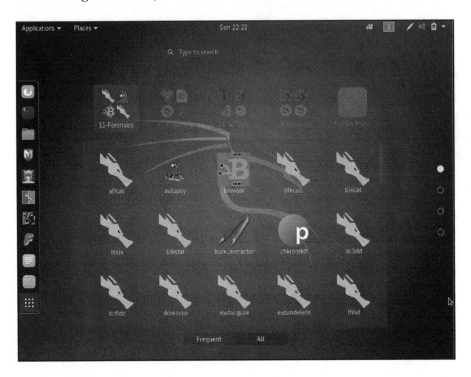

You'll notice that there are more tools available in this second option. This isn't to say that these are all the forensics tools available to us in Kali Linux. Many are available via the Terminal, some of which will be accessed in this manner, in later chapters.

I also encourage you to explore Kali Linux and it's many wonderful features that also make it a fully functional operating system, not just for use in forensics and penetration testing.

 Should you be interested in discovering more about Kali as a **penetration-testing (pen-testing)** distro, *Packt* has many detailed books on Kali Linux, which I wholeheartedly endorse. I own many of them in paperback and use them regularly on the job as well as for preparing my lectures.

Summary

In this chapter, we dived into the technical aspect of Kali Linux and discovered the types of modes available to us via the Kali Linux ISO image, whether running it from a live DVD, or installing it in a virtual environment. As well as being used as a live response forensic tool from a DVD, Kali can also be installed onto removable storage such as a flash drive or SD card. Being such a versatile operating system, we can also install Kali as a full-fledged operating system.

We also looked in depth at installing Kali Linux in a virtual environment using VirtualBox. For beginners, I'd definitely recommend this method of installation, as it allows for trial and error within an isolated environment. Be sure to allocate enough RAM, and also remember that the 32-bit version of Kali only allows up to 4 GB of RAM to be recognized and utilized. As a reminder, I once again suggest that you have access to both a Kali Linux live DVD and an installation of the OS, whether physical or virtual, to ensure that all bases are covered.

Understanding the forensics tools used in Kali is an excellent way to go about your investigations but we also need to understand the workings of storage media, file systems, data types, and locations. Join me in the next chapter, as we continue our journey into digital forensics by first understanding these fundamental concepts. See you in Chapter 3, *Understanding File Systems and Storage Media*.

3
Understanding Filesystems and Storage Media

It takes a lot more than just technical know-how to be a digital forensic investigator. There's a lot of research, processes, and analytics that also go into the case itself. Consider a scenario where you need to build a house. Sure, we need wood, nails, cement, metal, glass, and all other raw materials, and we also require the skilled laborers and contractors to construct the structure and piece it together. Apart from the materials, tools, and resources, we would have also done our research to ensure that we understood what is needed for this to be a successful project.

For instance, we would have had to obtain permits to build, perform soil analysis, consider the weather, and then choose to specify types of materials based on the weather, location, soil type, and so on. It goes without saying that there must be understanding of fundamental concepts in the field in order to efficiently carry out the task. In the same way, we need to have an understanding of the filesystems, operating systems, data types, and locations, as well as a thorough understanding of methods and procedures for preserving data, storage media, and general evidence.

In this chapter, we will learn about the following topics:

- The history of storage media
- Filesystems and operating systems
- What about the data?
- Data volatility
- The paging file and its importance in digital forensics

Storage media

The end result of any investigation is to prove whether something exists or took place. In laptops, desktops, mobile devices, and smart devices, data has to be stored somewhere, even if it's just temporarily. Most of us may be familiar with hard disk drives within laptops, desktops, mobile devices and so on, but we also need to focus on removable and portable storage devices. These include DVDs, portable drives, thumb or flash drives, SD and microSD cards, older media such as CDs and floppies, and countless more.

We should also consider that many portable flash drives come in many interesting shapes and sizes as novelty items, and may not take the usual shape of the ordinary rectangular-shaped drive. Another issue to consider is that many of these storage media devices have changed in size over the years and may be smaller in size, usually as a result of evolving technology.

IBM and the history of storage media

There can never be a story, journal, book, or even discussion on the history of hard drives and storage media without mentioning three letters: IBM . We're all familiar with this well-known tech giant, but we might not all be familiar with some of its great achievements.

International Business Machines, or **IBM** as we know it, has been around for quite some time. Known as the **Computing-Tabulating-Recording** (or **CTR) Company** back in the early 1900s, IBM is better known for building the very first hard disk drive, the first PC, its servers, desktops, and laptops.

Between the years 1956 and 1957, IBM made major inroads with the development and release of the 305 **RAMAC** (an acronym for **Random Access Method of Accounting and Control**), which utilized the first disk storage technology. This revolutionary technology weighed in at approximately one ton, and was roughly 16 square feet in size. The disk space capacity of this behemoth, however, was only 5 MB (megabytes - yes, I said *megabytes*) in size.

Although 5 MB by today's standard is roughly the size of a high-definition photo taken with a mobile device, all things considered, this really was a monumental achievement for its time. Before IBM's invention, data was stored on punch cards that could amount to as many as millions of cards just to hold a few megabytes.

A major issue faced back then with the introduction of this digital storage was the size of the device. Transportation by plane and truck may not have been an option for many; the space to store this would also have been an issue.

As technology progressed, IBM announced a much more portable computer in 1975, released as the IBM 5100 Portable Computer. In the 1980s, specifically 1981, we saw the birth of the IBM Personal Computer. Weighing in at much less than its predecessor, this portable computer also had a much more affordable price tag of between $8000 and $20,000 USD.

It wasn't until 1981 when IBM released the first personal computer that portability of computers was becoming an actual reality. With a price tag of $1,565, owners were afforded a keyboard and mouse, with options for a monitor, printer, and floppy drives. Apart from the floppy drives, this was the standard for today's personal computers.

Along with this newer and more portable technology, there were also improvements in data storage media over the years, which saw advancements from magnetic tape storage, to floppy disks and diskettes, CDs, DVDs, Blu-ray disks, and, of course, mechanical and solid-state drives.

Removable storage media

Continuing with our topic of storage media, I'd first like to start by discussing removable storage media, as they play a role just as important as that of fixed storage media in today's world.

Magnetic tape drives

Introduced by IBM in the 1950s, **magnetic tape** was an easy and very fast way to store data at a speed equal to its processing time. The IBM 726 magnetic tape reader and recorder was one of the first devices to offer this storage, with a capacity or tape density of 100 bits per linear inch of tape. *Inch of tape* should give an indicator of the size of the tape, which was wound on a large wheel, similar to old film roll movie tape.

With magnetic tape media, data is written across the width of the magnetic-coated plastic strip in frames separated by gaps consisting of blocks. Magnetic tape is still very much used today, and like many other storage media types has significantly decreased in size while increasing capacity and speed.

To give an idea of how far magnetic tape storage has come as of 2017, IBM has developed newer tape storage media with a tape density of 200 Gbps per inch on a single cartridge, which can record up to 333 GB of data. These cartridges (for older folks like myself) are the size of a cassette tape, or (for the younger ones) not much smaller than the average smartphone, which fits in your hand.

Floppy disks

The **floppy disk**, introduced yet again by IBM, was first seen along with its floppy disk drive in 1971. Although mainframe computers back then already had hard drives and magnetic tape storage media, there was the need for a simple and cheaper means of saving and passing on software and instructions to the mainframes, previously done using the much slower punch cards.

At the core of the floppy disk was a small magnetic disk which, although far more portable than magnetic tape storage and hard disk drives at the time, stored much less than other media we've mentioned.

Evolution of the floppy disk

Size: 8-inch

Year introduced: 1971

Maximum capacity: 80 KB (Kilobytes)

Size: 5.25-inch

Year introduced: 1976

Maximum capacity: 360 KB

Size: 3.5-inch

Year introduced: 1984

Maximum capacity: 1.2 MB (Megabytes)

 In 1986, the capacity of the floppy was increased to 1.44 MB, which remained as such until it was discontinued by Sony (the last remaining manufacturer of the floppy) in 2011.

Optical storage media

Optical storage media is so called because of the way in which data is written to the various media types involving the use of different types of lasers on the surface of the disk itself.

Although it may be somewhat difficult to distinguish various optical disks in the event that there are no default labels on them, they do have slightly varying differences in color and hue due to the size of lasers used in writing data to them.

Compact disks

Compact disks (or **CDs**) are made of pits and lands noticeable as bumps on the underside of the disk, coated with a thin layer of aluminum that results in a reflective surface. Data is written in concentric circles further split up into sectors of 512 bytes, each known as **tracks** on the CD from inside to outside (or edge) of the disk:

- **Diameter**: 120 millimeters
- **Type of laser used to write data**: 780 nm (nanometer) infrared laser
- **Maximum capacity of a CD**: 650-700 MB

Various types of CDs:

- **Compact Disk - Read-Only Memory (CD-ROM)**: This disk comes with data on it in the form of programs, games, music, and so on, and can only be read from
- **Compact Disk Recordable (CD-R)**: Data can be written to this disk, but only once
- **Compact Disk - ReWritable (CD-RW)**: Data can be written to this disk many times

Digital versatile disks

Digital versatile disks (or **DVDs**), although the same size in diameter, can store much more data than CDs:

- **Diameter**: 120 millimeters (same as a CD)
- **Type of laser used to write data**: 650 nm (nanometer) red laser
- **Maximum capacity of a DVD**: 4.7 GB (Gigabytes) and 15.9 GB (dual-layer DVD)

Various types of DVDs:

- **Digital Versatile Disk - Read-Only Memory (DVD-ROM)**: DVD comes with data already written to it, much like a CD-ROM.
- **Digital Versatile Disk - Recordable (DVD-R)**: Data can be written once to the DVD.

- **Digital Versatile Disk +Recordable (DVD+R)**: Data can be written once to the DVD. +R DVDs utilizes more advanced error detection and management technology.
- **Digital Versatile Disk -ReWritable (DVD-RW)**: Data can be written to the DVD several times.
- **Digital Versatile Disk - Recordable Dual Layer (DVD-R DL)**: DVD contains dual layers resulting in higher storage capacities between 7.95 GB on a DVD-9 disk, and 15.9 GB on a DVD-18 disk.
- **Digital Versatile Disk - Recordable Dual Layer (DVD+R DL)**: Same as the DVD-R DL, but has been argued as being the more efficient format, resulting in fewer errors.
- **Digital Versatile Disk - Random-Access Memory (DVD-RAM)**: Mainly used in video recording equipment due to its resiliency (lasting up to two decades) and the ability to rewrite data onto it. This disk is more expensive than other DVD formats, and is also not compatible with many common DVD drives and players.

Blu-ray disk

The current standard for removable disk media, the **Blu-ray disk** gets its name from the color of the laser used to read from and write to the disk. Due to the high-capacity storage of Blu-ray disks, **high definition (HD)** content can easily be stored on Blu-ray disks without loss of quality:

- **Diameter**: 120 millimeters (same as a CD and DVD)
- **Type of laser used to write data**: 405 nm (nanometer) blue laser
- **Maximum capacity of a DVD**: 27 GB (Gigabytes) and 50 GB (double-layer Blu-ray)

Flash storage media

Flash memory is so named because the data is written to and erased from using electrical charges. You may have perhaps heard someone say that they've had to *flash* their mobile device. This is quite similar to erasing flash storage media on smartphones and smart devices, except devices with operating systems such as Android and iOS require a much more extensive procedure for flashing and reinstalling their operating systems. The end result, however, is very much the same in that the memory and storage areas are reset or wiped.

Flash storage chips come in two types, known as NAND and NOR flash memory, and are responsible for high-speed and high-capacity storage of data on flash storage media. They are newer types of **EEPROM** chips (an acronym for **Electrically Erasable Programmable Read-Only Memory**), and instead can wipe blocks of data or the entire drive, rather than just one byte at a time, as with the slower EEPROM. This type of flash memory chip is non-volatile, meaning that the data is still stored on the chip even after power to the chip is lost. Data is erased when specific instructions are sent to the chip in the form of electrical signals via a method known as **in-circuit writing,** which alters the data accordingly.

The following picture shows one of my old 1 GB flash drives with a Samsung NAND chip, which stores the data. If you'd like to get down into the technical details of the chip, you can have a look at the datasheet PDF at `http://datasheet.iiic.cc/datasheets-1/samsung_` `semiconductor_division/K9K4G08U0M-PCB00.pdf`:

Flash media storage has so far become the ultimate in portability, with many types ranging from the size of your thumb to the size of your nail on your little finger. The lifespan of flash storage all depends on the usage, as they all have an average read-write usage, sometimes displayed on the packaging of the device. The read-write speeds are also some of the fastest at this point, which is why hard disk drives have moved away from the traditional mechanical disk mechanism to a solid-state one. More on SSD will be discussed later in this chapter.

With flash storage media capacities ranging from 2 GB to 256 GB particularly on SD, microSD and flash drives, these can now act as very fast removable drives with operating systems installed on them, and can even be partitioned using various tools. Yes indeed, Kali Linux most certainly can be installed onto a flash drive, SD or microSD card (and be made bootable) with as little as 8 GB of storage space.

USB flash drives

The **Universal Serial Bus (USB)** port or interface, released in 1995, has become the standard for all devices, replacing older devices that would have connected to specific parallel ports on a computer. It's quite common to see almost any device or peripherals connected to a computer via a USB connection including mice, keyboards, flash drives, printers, scanners, cameras, mobile devices, and just about every other device.

Evolution of the USB port:

USB version	Released year	Data transfer speed
USB 1.0 and 1.1	1995	12 Mbps
USB 2.0	2000	480 Mbps
USB 3.0	2008	5 GBps
USB 3.1	2013	10 GBps

USB flash drives come in all shapes and sizes today, from the standard rectangular shape to every imaginable. USB flash drives use NAND EEPROM chips to store their data, and today are available in various versions that define the read/write speeds of the flash drive.

The following picture shows various flash drives ranging from oldest to newest, left to right. The first three drives are all USB 2.1; however, the first two are 8 GB flash drives, and the third, which is significantly smaller, is a 32 GB flash drive. The fourth drive (Corsair) is a 64 GB USB 3.1 drive:

I should give special mention to the elephant in the room here, being the novelty flash drive, which can easily pass as a keychain or toy, and may actually pose a threat to organizations that do not allow employees to bring to work or leave with flash drives due to the sensitive nature of the data within the organization.

Flash memory cards

Like flash drives, **flash memory cards** (or memory cards, as they are fondly referred to) also use NAND flash memory, which, as we previously learned, is non-volatile, solid-state memory. Unlike USB flash drives, however, these cards do not come with a USB interface and must be used with either an adapter or memory card reader.

Over the years and decades even, we've had several formats of memory cards grace our desktops, laptops, mobiles, and other devices, including cameras, MP3 players, and even toys. Although I'll only cover some of the more popular cards of today, it is important that you are at least familiar with memory cards and are also able to identify them.

Flash memory card types:

- **Memory Stick PRO Duo (MSPD**, proprietary card developed by Sony)
- **Secure Digital (SD)**
- **MicroSD**
- **Compact Flash (CF)**
- **MultiMediaCard (MMC)**
- **xD-Picture (xD)**
- **Smart Media (SM)**

Of the above-mentioned, I've opted to show three from my collection in the following picture. The card to the left being a Sony Memory Stick PRO Duo. The card to the middle is an SD card that has a sliding lock to the side, used to prevent data from being overwritten. The card to the right is the more common card today, the microSD:

I'd like to do a brief comparison of the PRO Duo (card to the left), SD (middle), and the microSD card (right side). Developed at least a decade apart, the older PRO Duo card is larger, with a capacity of 2 GB. Although not seen on the SD card, its capacity is 4 GB, and the smallest and newest card to the right (microSD) actually has a whopping 64 GB of storage capacity.

Have a look at the following image to get a close-up of the microSD card. It shows the capacity of 64 GB, and also the class of the microSD card (Class 10). 64 GB of data on something as small as a finger nail! Still, microSD cards are being developed with even larger capacities of 128 GB and even 256 GB:

The various classes of microSD cards identifies their read/write speeds and suggested uses. I do suggest getting a Class 10 microSD card if purchasing one, as the C10 is much faster than the other classes (2, 4, and 6) and supports constant HD and even 4k video recording.

As mentioned earlier, flash memory cards require card readers, which connect to laptops, desktops, and other media players using USB ports. The following picture shows one of my many card readers, which supports Compact Flash, Memory Stick PRO Duo, Secure Digital, and even the Smart Media cards:

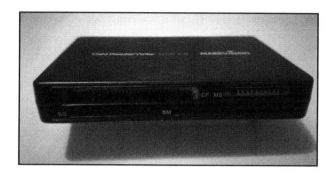

Hard disk drives

Now that we've had a good look at non-volatile storage including tape storage and flash storage, lets go a bit deeper into the world of hard disk drives, which serve as fixed storage media. I'll try to keep things simple and short by focusing mainly on the knowledge necessary for forensics investigators in particular.

Hard disk drive technology has certainly come a long way from the monstrous storage devices first seen in IBM mainframes, and are now more compact, faster, and more affordable, with capacities in the terabytes.

Although the newer solid-state drives use the same type of memory found in flash memory devices, they are still a bit costly when compared to mechanical drives. This perhaps may be one of the contributing factors when wondering why older mechanical drive technology is still being used. Mechanical drives consist of moving parts including platters, an actuator arm, and a very powerful magnet. Although it is very common to still find these mechanical HDDs in today's laptops and hard drives, they are much slower than the newer solid-state drives, which have no moving parts and look very similar to the chipset of a USB flash drive.

In your forensics investigations and adventures, you may come across or be presented with older HDDs that can have different interfaces and use different cable technologies to connect to motherboards. Let's have a look, shall we?

IDE HDDs

Many of the first PCs in the mid 1980s were outfitted with hard drives that used **PATA** (an acronym for **Parallel Advanced Technology Attachment**) and **IDE** (an acronym for **Integrated Drive Electronics**) technology. As with all older devices back then, parallel transmission was the order of the day, allowing for very limited throughput. An easy way to identify older IDE drives is to simply have a look at the interface where the data and power cables connect to the drive.

These older drives, as seen in the following image, have four pins for power, which connect to a Molex connector, separated by eight pins used to set the device as a master or slave device, and then 40 pins for the IDE data cable, which transmits the data to the motherboard:

In 1994, advancements in technology led to the release of **EIDE** (an acronym for **Enhanced Integrated Drive Electronics**), which saw an increase in the number of pins for the data cable from 40 to 80, also increasing the transmission speeds from 4 Mbps to a possible 133 Mbps.

IDE/EIDE were still, however, limited to a maximum of four IDE/EIDE drives per computer, as the jumper pins on the drive only allowed for two primary and two secondary drives, set in a master and slave configuration. Consideration also had to be given to the fact that CD-ROM and RW devices and DVD-ROM and RW devices were also using IDE/EIDE technology at that time.

SATA HDDs

In 2002, Seagate released an HDD technology called **SATA** (an acronym for **Serial Advanced Technology Attachment**), which used serial transmission instead of slower parallel transmission. Whereas PATA drives speeds of 33/66/133 Mbps, SATA drives boasted speeds of 150/300/600 Mbps. This meant that the lowest SATA transmission speed of 150 Mbps was faster than the highest PATA speed of 133 Mbps.

The connector interfaces of the SATA drives were also different, but it was common at the time to see SATA drives with connectors for both SATA and PATA power cables for backward compatibility.

SATA data cables are much thinner than PATA cables, as they only contain seven wires connecting to seven pins. SATA devices use one cable per drive, unlike PATA devices, which connect two drives on one IDE/EIDE cable connected in a master/slave configuration.

The following image shows an older SATA drive with SATA data and power connectors to the right, and a legacy IDE Molex power cable (four pins) to the left:

SATA still continues to be standard today for drive technology for both desktops and laptops, and has had several revisions as listed here. Speeds listed are in MBps and not Mbps:

- **SATA 1**: 150 MBps
- **SATA 2**: 300 MBps
- **SATA 3**: 600 MBps

The following image shows two SATA laptop 2.5-inch drives. The one to the left is damaged, and has been opened for us to see the circular platter at the middle with the actuator arm at the top, slightly positioned over the platter. At the end of the actuator arm is a read/write head, which actually does the reading and the writing of data to the platter.

The drive to the right in the image is actually a hybrid drive, or an **SSHD** (an acronym for **Solid-State Hybrid Drive**). This is actually a mechanical drive like the one to the left, but also has flash memory in it to allow for faster access to the data on the platters:

Solid-state drives

As briefly mentioned before, SSDs are non-volatile storage media, and use NAND flash memory in an array to hold data. SSDs have been around for quite some time; however, mainstream use would have been greatly hampered by the high cost of the drive. Samsung first released a 32 GB SSD with a PATA interface in 1996, followed by SanDisk's 32 GB SSD, but with a SATA interface.

Although SSD drives use flash memory, the materials used are more high-end than that found in flash drives, which makes it highly preferred for use as a hard drive, but again, contributes to the very high cost.

Some advantages of SSDs come from the fact that there are no moving parts in an SSD. No moving parts makes the SSD more durable in the event of a fall or swift foot to the PC tower, as there are no platters or actuator arms to be scratched or struck. Also, the faster read/ write speeds and access times greatly reduce the time taken for the device to boot or start, and even gives an enhanced experience when using resource-intensive software and games.

As far as digital forensics go, SSDs are still a relatively new technology that will be constantly improved upon for some time to come. It's important to remember that you are not dealing with a mechanical drive, and to remember that data on an SSD, much like a flash drive or memory card, can be lost or wiped within minutes or even seconds. Although traditional tools can be used to image and recover data from SSDs, I strongly suggest on researching any SSD drive before performing any forensic activities, to get a better understanding of its workings and complexities such as dechipping and wear-leveling algorithms.

Filesystems and operating systems

Now that we've covered the physical, let's get logical! Any and every type of storage media needs to be formatted with a particular filesystem. The filesystem chosen will also determine which operating system can be installed on the medium, along with file and partition sizes.

A simple way to think of this is to imagine a blank sheet of paper as any type of new or wiped storage media. We can put several types of information on this piece of paper, but we'll probably first want to organize or prepare the sheet of paper in a way that makes our data easy to understand, access, and even store. We can choose to write on it, from left to right in sentences and paragraphs in English, or we can perhaps create tables, using rows and columns. We can even use printed slides to display our data, or even use images, graphs, and flowcharts. Additionally, we can format your storage media in a way that best suits the data that will be stored and used.

Filesystems ensure that the data is organized in such a way that it can be easily recognized and indexed. Consider the storage space within a filing cabinet with multiple compartments. Some may be used specifically for storing files in alphabetical order, others in chronological order, some compartments for stationery supplies, miscellaneous, and even random items. Although all used for storing different items, they can all be labeled and easily recognized, and also organized in such a way where the contents of each compartment can be easily accessed or even removed.

To install any operating system on a hard drive or removable storage media, the device must first be formatted and prepared for the operating system by choosing the appropriate filesystem. Windows, macOS, Android, Kali, and so on all have filesystems that organize the storage medium so that the OS can be successfully installed.

Some of the more popular operating systems and their filesystems are:

- **Microsoft Windows**:
    - **Filesystem**: NTFS (**Net Technology File System**)
    - **Supported versions**: Windows 10, 8, 7, Vista, XP, 2000, NT
    - **Maximum volume size**: 16 **EB** (**Exabytes**)
    - **Maximum supported file size**: 256 TB
    - **NTFS features**: Compression, **EFS** (**Encrypted File System**), disk quotas

 Older versions of Microsoft Windows supported the **FAT** (**File Allocation System**) filesystem by default. Newer versions of Windows also support FAT and FAT32, but with drive size limitations (8 TB) and file size limitations (4 GB). exFAT was created to remove the limitations of FAT32, but may not be as widely supported as FAt32.

- **Macintosh (macOS)**:
    - **Filesystem**: HFS+ (**Hierarchical File System**)
    - **Supported versions**: macOS up until version 10
    - **Maximum volume size**: 2 TB
    - **Maximum supported file size**: 2 GB

 At the time of this writing, Apple has advanced to a newer filesystem called **APFS** (**Apple File System**) to replace HFS+, optimized specifically for SSDs. APFS will be available in macOS 10.12.4 and iOS 10.3.

- **Linux**:
    - **Filesystem**: Ext4 (**Fourth Extended File System**). Several filesystems are available for Linux, but I recommend this one if you are uncertain as to which should be used
    - **Supported versions**: RedHat, Kali, Ubuntu, and so on
    - **Maximum volume size**: 1 EB
    - **Maximum supported file size**: 16 TB

Many open source operating system distros are based on Linux including Kali Linux and Android, and so use the ext2/ext3/ext 4 filesystems. They are also able to use the FAT32 filesystem.
FAT32 can be used across any platform, including older versions of Windows, Mac, and Linux, and is supported by almost any device with a USB port.

What about the data?

In this chapter so far, we've looked at the various media for storing data. Now I'd like to talk about the actual data itself, some of its states, and what happens when it's accessed.

Data states

Firstly, there's **data in transit**, also called **data in motion**. These simply describe data on the move, perhaps traversing across the network between devices or even between storage media, actively moving between locations.

Then there's **data in use**. Data in this state is currently being accessed by a user, or processed by a CPU. When data is accessed or used, it's pulled from the hard drive and temporarily stored in RAM, which is much faster than the hard drive (particularly mechanical drives) and stored there for as long as the user accesses it and there is power to the device.

When data is not in motion or transit, nor in use, it is described as **data at rest**. In this state, the data *rests* or resides on non-volatile media such as hard drives, optical media, flash drives, and memory cards.

Metadata

Metadata is simply data about data. Take an item such as a laptop stored in a warehouse, for example. Somewhere in the warehouse (and also possibly in other locations such as the cloud) there may be several pieces of information about that laptop that can be referred to as data about the laptop, or even laptop metadata, such as:

- Location of the laptop within the warehouse
- Laptop brand and model
- Manufacture date

- Warranty dates and information
- Hardware and software specs
- Color and size

Additionally, data may have at least some basic information about it, whether it be at rest or in motion. At rest, data may be indexed on a hard drive in the file table to identify the location of the data and whether it may be available to the user, or is waiting to be overwritten. Data in transit will also contain header information (which will be discussed in later chapters), which gives information about source and destination addresses and the size of the data, just to name a couple.

Slack space

Clusters are the smallest amount of disk space or allocation units on storage media, which store data. When formatting drives, we need to define the size of these allocation units, or we can use the default cluster size of 4 Kilobytes. This is where Slack space comes in.

Slack space is the empty and unused space within clusters that contain data, but are not completely filled with data. To fully understand this, we first need to understand default cluster sizes specified by operating systems. A drive formatted using NTFS (for Windows) has a default cluster size or 4 KB. Let's say that you've saved a text file to your disk with a file size of 3 KB. This means that you still have 1 KB of unused or slack space within that cluster.

Slack space is of particular interest to a forensic investigator as data can be easily hidden in slack space. Luckily for us, we have several tools available, such as **Sleuth Kit** and **Autopsy**, within Kali Linux, to help investigate slack space and find hidden files.

Data volatility

In this section, we take a look at why data is lost when power to the volatile memory is lost.

Data can exist as long as the media it is stored on is capable of storing the data. Hard drives (mechanical and solid-state), flash drives, and memory cards are all non-volatile storage media. Although SSDs have and continue to make drastic improvements in data access times, RAM thus far remains the faster type of memory, typically referred to only as **memory**, inside devices.

RAM, however, is **volatile memory**. Unlike non-volatile memory found in hard drives and flash drives, data stored in RAM is kept there temporarily, only for as long as there is an electrical current being provided to the chips. There are two types of RAM that we need to be aware of: **Static RAM (SRAM)** and **Dynamic RAM (DRAM)**.

SRAM is superior to DRAM, but is far more costly than DRAM because of the extensive materials used in building the chips. SRAM is also physically much larger than DRAM. SRAM can be found in the CPU cache (**L1** or **Level 1**) and on some chips on the motherboard (**L2/L3**), although in very small sizes (KB) due to the cost and physical size.

Although DRAM is slower, it is much cheaper and remains one of the reasons for its use as main memory in devices. What makes RAM volatile is its components, such as **transistors** and **capacitors**. Some of you may already be familiar with this topic from certification courses such as **A+**, but for the benefit of all our readers, allow me to go into a bit more detail.

DRAM uses capacitors, which store electrical charges temporarily as part of a refresh circuit. The chips need to be constantly refreshed in order to hold the data while being accessed. However, between refreshes, a wait-state is created, which makes DRAM slower when compared to SRAM as it uses transistors instead of capacitors, which do not have wait-states.

Over the decades, there have been many types of DRAM or memory sticks in slightly varying sizes and increased pins with which to make contact with the motherboard. Some of the RAM types in order of age are:

- **Extended Data Output RAM (EDO RAM)**: One of the earlier types of DRAM.
- **Synchronous Dynamic RAM (SDRAM)**: Began synchronizing itself with the CPU clock speed. Maximum transfer rate of 133 MT/s (Millions of transfers per second). Labelled as PC100, PC133, PC166.
- **DDR-SDRAM/DDR** 1 (**Double Data Rate - SDRAM**): Effectively doubled the transfer rate of SD RAM. Maximum transfer rate of 400 MT/s.
- DDR2: Maximum transfer rate of 800 MT/s.
- DDR3: Consumes up to a third less power than DDR2. Maximum transfer rate of 1600 MT/s.
- DDR4: Maximum transfer rate of 3200 MT/s.

In today's laptops and desktops, one might mainly come across DDR3 and DDR4, but it may not be uncommon to run into a legacy machine with DD2 or (miraculously) DDR1. The following image shows different RAM types **DIMM (Dual Inline Memory Modules)** from top to bottom, SDRAM (top), DDR1, DDR2, and lastly DDR3:

 Laptops also use DDR RAM, but are available in a more compact size called **SODIMM (Small Outline DIMM)** modules.

The paging file and its importance in digital forensics

Operating systems have the ability to use a portion of the hard disk as an extension of RAM. This is referred to as **virtual memory,** and is usually a good idea if a computer or laptop has limited RAM. Although the hard drive is much slower than the RAM, the swap file or paging file on the disk can store files and programs that are being accessed less, leaving the RAM available to store data being frequently accessed. This process involves the OS swapping pages of data less frequently used, and moving data to the dedicated paging file area on the hard drive.

In forensics investigations, the paging file is very important to us. Although not as volatile as RAM itself due to being stored on the hard disk, it is a hidden file in Windows called `pagefile.sys`, and should always be inspected using tools of your choice, as this file may reveal passwords for encrypted areas, information from sites visited, documents opened, logged-in users, printed items, and so on.

Data on mechanical drives, in particular, are stored in a fragmented manner; however, the advantage of the paging or swap file is that the data can be stored in a contiguous manner, one piece after the next, allowing for faster access times.

It is recommended that the size of the paging file is set to 1.5 times the amount of memory, and also be stored on a separate drive if possible, not just a separate partition.

 `Pagefile.sys` can be located in the Windows registry path: `HKEY_LOCAL_MACHINE\SYSTEM\CurrentControlSet\Control\Sessi on Manager\Memory Management`.

Summary

In this chapter, we took the time to cover some of the basics about non-volatile storage media, which stores data even after there is no power supplied to the medium. Non-volatile media includes different types of hard disk drives, such as mechanical and solid-state PATA and SATA drives, flash drives, and memory cards.

Newer storage media devices including SSDs use a special type of flash memory called NAND flash to store data. This flash memory is by far faster and more durable than traditional mechanical drives, as the devices contain no moving parts; however, they are still quite costly for now.

We also had a look at various filesystems associated with various operating systems, and saw that the smallest allocation of data is called a Cluster, in which can reside slack space. Slack space is unused space within a cluster, in which data can be hidden. Data itself has different states and can be at rest, in motion, or in use. Regardless of the state of the data, there always resides some information about the data itself, called metadata.

Any data accessed by the user or OS is temporarily stored in volatile memory or RAM. Although data can be stored for lengthy periods on non-volatile memory, it is lost when electrical charges to volatile memory (RAM) are also lost. An area of the hard disk called the paging file can act as virtual RAM, allowing the computer to think it has more RAM than installed.

I do encourage you to do more research and expand your knowledge on these topics, allowing you to gain more understanding of what was covered. Let's now move on to the next chapter, where we'll learn about investigative procedures and best practices for incident response, such as acquiring volatile data and procedures for working with and analyzing live machines.

4

Incident Response and Data Acquisition

It's sometimes difficult to ascertain exactly what qualifies as evidence, especially at the exact start of an investigation when all the facts on what occurred may not have yet been collected or stated. As in any investigation, we should be aware of and follow the guidelines, practices, and procedures for acquiring evidence in such a way that it is not tampered with or in a worst-case scenario, lost.

At the scene of a crime, let's say a shooting, there are specific items that may immediately qualify as evidence. The physical evidence is easily collected, put into evidence bags, labeled, and then shipped off to the labs and secure storage areas for safekeeping. This evidence may include spent bullet casings, perhaps a gun, fingerprints, and blood samples. Let's not forget witness statements and **CCTV** (an acronym for **Closed Circuit Television**) footage also. It's also of interest to consider the individuals from law enforcement agencies that would be at the scene, and the order in which they may have arrived. Seems simple enough.

When a breach or crime involving a computer or smart device is reported, however, collecting the evidence is sometimes not as simple as there are many factors to consider before labeling any items as evidence.

If a desktop was involved in the act for example, do we take the tower alone or do we also seize the monitor, keyboard, mouse, and speakers? What about the other peripherals such as printers and scanners? Are there any additional fixed or removable storage media at the scene and do we also seize them?

This chapter answers all these questions and provides guidelines and best practices for incident response, evidence acquisition, and other topics, including:

- Digital evidence acquisition procedures
- Preserving evidence integrity
- Write blocking and hashing
- Powered-on versus powered-off device acquisition
- Live acquisition best practices
- Data imaging and hashing
- Chain of custody

Digital evidence acquisitions and procedures

As we covered in the last chapter, data can be stored on both fixed and removable storage media. Data, however, can easily be deleted or completely lost depending on a multitude of factors that must be considered if we are to ensure the preservation of data. It might even be argued that there are more threats to digital storage than paper-based. The following are some comparisons of threats to both:

- Threats to paper-based storage include:
  - Water
  - Fire and humidity
  - Bugs
  - Age
  - Natural disasters—floods, earthquakes, tornadoes, hurricanes, and so on
- Threats to data on storage media include:
  - Human-error and negligence
  - Magnetism and electromagnetic fields
  - Water and condensation
  - Heat
  - Dust

- Impact
- Voltage
- Static electricity
- Natural disasters—floods, earthquakes, tornadoes, hurricanes, and so on

When exactly does data become evidence? Specific data may have a value that is relative to an investigation when considering the events that transpired.

Incident response and first responders

Preserving evidence does not begin only at the acquisition of data, but as early on as the physical viewing of the suspect device. There should be some kind of structured response to the suspected crime or breach in the same way as with a crime reported to the police. In the same way, a person makes a call to the emergency services who then dispatch the police, fire services, and ambulance personnel and other first responders who may then escalate the issue to the FBI or other agencies. There should also be a similar chain of command when dealing with reports that require digital investigation.

When a breach or crime is discovered or suspected, there should be a dedicated first responder who is alerted and called to the scene. This person usually has some knowledge or understanding of the workings of devices, networks, and even of the IT infrastructure in the organization if applicable.

First responder personnel can include:

- Systems administrators
- Network administrators
- Security administrators
- IT managers

While the people in the preceding roles may not be skilled in digital forensics or digital investigations, they will be responsible for securing the scene and ensuring that the data, peripherals, equipment, and storage are not used, tampered with, removed, or compromised by unauthorized individuals.

Duties of first responders include:

- Being the first to respond to the scene (as the name suggests) and making an initial assessment
- Documenting the scene and room fully in a circular fashion using the center of the room as a focal point
- Securing the scene by not allowing unauthorized users or suspects, access to the devices or area, and especially to volatile data and storage media
- Preserving and packaging evidence for transportation, ensuring the use of the **Chain of Custody (CoC)** forms

Documentation and evidence collection

Documentation of the scene should also be done by the first responders to aid in investigations. Documentation of the scene should include photographs, video, voice recording, and manual documentation of the following:

- Room that the device is located in (desk, ceiling, entrance/exit, windows, lighting, electrical outlets, and data drops)
- State of the device (on, off, power light blinking)
- Screen contents, if the device is on (operating system, running programs, date and time, wired and/or wireless network connectivity)
- Books, notes, pieces of paper
- Connected and disconnected cables

Once the scene has been secured and documented by the first responders, the forensic investigator should also be called in, if not already alerted.

If the first responder has been trained in evidence collection and preservation, they can also begin the process of acquiring what can be considered as physical evidence.

Examples of physical evidence include:

- **Computer towers.**
- **Laptops.**
- **Tablets.**

- **Fixed and removable storage media**: Hard drives, optical media, tape storage, memory cards, card readers, adapters, docking stations, printers, scanners, mobile phones, and iPods. Media and MP3 players and other devices that may have been used in carrying out the breach. Routers and switches may also contain evidence such as connectivity logs, source, and destination addresses, and even visited websites.
- **Cables and chargers**.

Physical evidence collection and preservation

Consideration should be given to the physical aspect of the evidence collection phase. Like any other investigation, documentation, collection, and preservation should be done while following proper guidelines and best practices to ensure the integrity of the investigation. At a crime scene, for example, evidence has to be properly identified, labeled as handled by authorized staff, and trained in investigative procedures that can be scrutinized in a court of law.

A first responder toolkit should contain the following items in preparation for documentation, evidence collection, and preservation at the scene:

- Protective clothing including eye-wear and gloves
- Anti-static mat or wristbands
- Identification label tags, stickers, and portable labeling devices (if available)
- Various pens and markers for easy identification
- Cable ties
- Toolkit with various sizes of Philip, Flat Head, Torx, and specialized screwdrivers or heads
- Flashlight and magnifying glasses
- Seizure and Chain of Custody forms
- Containers, boxes, and packaging materials including anti-static and stronghold bags

Here's a budget but portable and very well-organized screwdriver kit that I keep in my first responder toolkit. It has all the attachments for opening desktops, laptops, tablets, and also for removing and even opening removable storage media such as hard disk drives, optical drives, and even floppy drives if I encounter them:

Physical acquisition tools

We've looked at the tools necessary for the collection and acquisition of physical evidence, but what tools do we need for the acquisition and extraction of digital evidence? Remember when we covered the different types of storage media back in Chapter 3, *Understanding Filesystems and Storage Media*? We saw that many of them had their own connectors as they were of various sizes.

Here's a list of some of the equipment required when acquiring data from evidence:

- Write blocker (can also be software-based)
- Card reader
- Various adapters (USB to SATA and EIDE, USB to various types of USB)
- Device cables such as power, SATA, EIDE, HDMI, VGA
- Networking cables such as straight-through, crossover, console

The following image shows a collection of various USB adapters, all costing under $10, and they are all available on Amazon:

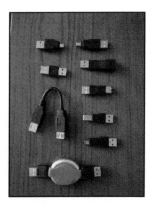

For laptop drives, I also use a SATA to USB 3.0 adapter, as seen here:

For connecting to routers and switches, console cables and serial to USB cables can also be included in your kit, like the ones seen here:

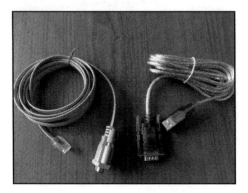

All mobile devices including phones and tablets can also connect to laptops and desktops via USB ports. The following image shows an OTG cable, which can connect a USB device to phones or tablets with OTG capabilities:

Guidelines for physical collection and preservation:

- Label all cables and connectors
- Use labeled evidence collection bags as needed
- Special stronghold bags may have to be used when storing devices with wireless and radio capabilities, preventing communication with other devices
- Store sensitive equipment such as hard drives and flash drives in anti-static bags and protective casings
- Label containers used for storage during transportation
- Maintain the Chain of Custody forms when passing evidence from one person/handler to another (discussed later in this chapter)

Order of volatility

When collecting evidence, we should keep in mind the volatility of data. As mentioned earlier in this chapter, data can be easily lost or destroyed. As such, when collecting data, a well-documented and common best practice would be to collect evidence in the order of most volatile to the least volatile if possible.

The **Scientific Working Group on Digital Evidence** (**SWGDE**) capture of live systems document, lists the order of volatility from most to least volatile and crucial as follows:

- RAM
- Running processes
- Active network connections
- System settings
- Storage media

Chain of Custody

The Chain of Custody is a form that legally ensures the integrity of evidence as it is exchanged between individuals, and so it also provides a level of accountability as personal identification is required when completing the forms. This form gives an exact log and account of the transportation and the exchange between parties, from a collection at the scene to a presentation in a court.

Some of the typical fields on the Chain of Custody form are:

- Case number
- Offence
- Victim and suspect names
- Date and time seized:
    - Location when seized
    - Item number
    - Description of item
    - Signatures and IDs of individuals releasing and receiving the items
- Authorization for disposal
- Witness to destruction of evidence
- Release to lawful owner

The sample Chain of Custody form can be downloaded directly from the **National Institute of Standards and Technology (NIST):**

```
https://www.nist.gov/document/sample-chain-custody-formdocx
```

Powered-on versus powered-off device acquisition

When investigating devices that are powered on and powered off, special consideration must be given to the volatility of data. Booting, rebooting, or shutting down a device can cause data to be written to the hard drive or even lost within RAM and the paging file.

Powered-on devices

When investigating a powered-on device the following precautions should be taken:

- Move the mouse or glide your fingers across the touchpad if you suspect the device may be in a *sleep* state. Do not click on the buttons as this may open or close programs and processes.
- Photograph and record the screen and all visible programs, data, time, and desktop items.
- Unplug the power cord on desktops and remove the battery, if possible, on portables.

It is of utmost important that data stored in RAM and paging files be collected with as little modification to the data as possible. More on this will be covered in later chapters using imaging tools such as Guymager and DC3DD in Kali Linux. Other live acquisition tools such as C.A.I.N.E and Helix can also be used for acquiring RAM and the paging file.

There are quite a few reasons for imaging and acquiring the RAM. As mentioned in the previous chapter, data that may have been encrypted by the user may be stored in an unencrypted state of RAM. Logged in users, opened programs, accessed files, and running processes can all be extracted and analyzed if the RAM and paging file are analyzed. However, if the device is switched off or rebooted, this data and evidence can easily be lost.

For powered-on portable and powered-on devices, the battery should be removed, if possible. Some devices, however, may not have a removable battery. In these cases, the power button should be held down for 30 to 40 seconds, which forces the device to power off.

Powered-off devices

Powered-off devices should never be turned on unless done so by the forensic investigator. Special steps must be taken to ensure that existing data is not erased and that new data is not written.

Devices can often seem as if they are off, but they can be in a sleep or hibernate state. As a simple test, the mouse can be moved and monitors (if any) can be switched on to determine if they are in fact in either of those states. Even if they are in an off state, one should still photograph the screen and ports.

When investigating portable and mobile devices in an already off state, it is suggested that the battery is removed (if possible) and placed in an evidence bag to ensure that there will be no accidental way to turn the device on once unplugged. According to the *NIST.SP.800-101r1—Guidelines on Mobile Forensics*, it should be noted that removing the battery can alter contents in volatile memory, even when in an off state.

Write blocking

Once our evidence has been properly documented and collected, we can begin working on acquiring the actual digital evidence. I'll mention this a couple times in an effort to drive home the point, but the original evidence should only be used to create forensic copies or images, which will be discussed further on in this chapter and again in other chapters.

Working on the original evidence can and usually will modify the contents of the medium. For instance, booting a seized laptop into its native OS will allow data to be written to the hard drive and may also erase and modify contents contained in the RAM and paging file.

To prevent this from happening, the use of a write blocker must be employed. Write blockers, as the name suggests, prevent data from being written to the evidence media. Write blockers can be found in both hardware and software types. If a hardware write blocker is not available, software versions are readily available as standalone features in forensic operating systems including C.A.I.N.E, as mentioned in Chapter 1, *Introduction to Digital Forensics*, and also as a part of some commercial and open source tools such as EnCase and Autopsy.

Again, it is of high importance that a write blocker be used in investigations to protect and preserve the original evidence from being modified. The following image shows a cheap and efficient portable SATA and IDE adapter with write-blocking switches, used in drive acquisition and recovery:

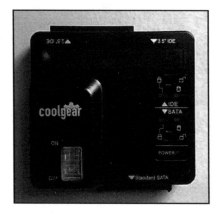

Data imaging and hashing

Imaging refers to the exact copying of data either as a file, folder, partition, or entire storage media or drive. When doing a regular copy of files and folders, not all files may be copied based on their attributes being set to the system or even hidden. To prevent files from being left out, we perform a special type of copy where every bit is copied or imaged exactly as it is on the current medium, as if taking a picture or snapshot of the data.

Creating a copy of each bit of data exactly as is, is referred to as a **Physical Image**. Performing a **Bitstream copy** ensures the integrity of the copy. To further prove this, a hash of the original evidence and the physical image are calculated and compared. If the copy is off by even one bit of data, the hash values will be quite different.

> The original evidence should only be handled by qualified and authorized professionals and should also only be used to create forensically sound physical images. The original evidence should otherwise never be used as this compromises integrity and the investigation.

Message Digest (MD5) hash

Hash values are produced by specific algorithms and are used to verify the integrity of the evidence by proving that the data was not modified. Hash values can be thought of as digital fingerprints in that they are unique and play a major role in the identification of evidence and physical images.

One such algorithm, although older and containing vulnerabilities, is the **Message Digest (MD5)** cryptographic hashing algorithm, which produces a 128-bit hexadecimal output value.

For a working example, let's open a browser and head over to `http://passwordsgenerator.net/md5-hash-generator/`.

This site creates hashes of words and sentences as strings. For this example, I've entered the string `Digital Forensics with Kali Linux` without the parentheses. The MD5 value automatically calculated was displayed as **7E9506C4D9DD85220FB3DF671F09DA35**, as seen in the following screenshot:

By removing the `K` from the `Kali`, from the same string that now reads `Digital Forensics with ali Linux`, the MD5 now reads **7A4C7AA85B114E91F247779D6A0B3022**, as seen in the following screenshot:

As a quick comparison, we can see that just removing the K from the Kali yields a noticeably different result:

- Digital Forensics with Kali Linux:
  7E9506C4D9DD85220FB3DF671F09DA35
- Digital Forensics with ali Linux:
  7A4C7AA85B114E91F247779D6A0B3022

I encourage you to try it yourself and also perhaps add a comma or period to the string to further compare hash values.

Secure Hashing Algorithm (SHA)

Another cryptographic hash algorithm commonly used in forensics and also used in the next chapter is SHA1. The **Secure Hashing Algorithm-1 (SHA1)** is more secure than MD5 as it produces a 160-bit output instead of a 128-bit output as with MD5. Due to known collision attacks against both MD5 and SHA-1, the safer and more robust option for hashing is now *SHA-2*.

SHA-2 is actually a group of hashes and not just one, as with SHA-1, with the most common bit-length being SHA-256 which produces a 256-bit output. Alternate bit-length algorithms of SHA-2 are SHA-224, SHA-384, and SHA-512.

The stronger the cryptographic algorithm used, the less chance of it being attacked or compromised. This means that the integrity of the evidence and physical images created remain intact, which will prove useful in forensic cases and expert testimony.

More on creating hashes will be demonstrated in Chapter 5, *Evidence Acquisition and Preservation with DC3DD and Guymager*, using DC3DD and Guymager.

Device and data acquisition guidelines and best practices

While I've tried to give you a general and summarized overview of the procedures when collecting and preserving evidence, there are several official documents that I highly recommend you read and become familiar with, as they all give good details and guidelines on documentation of the scene, evidence collection, and data acquisition.

The **SWGDE (Scientific Working Group on Digital Evidence)** *Best Practices for Computer Forensics, Version 3.1*, published in September 2014, outlines best practices for computer forensics in the following areas:

- Evidence collection and handling
- Evidence acquisition and transport
- Guidelines for investigating powered-on and powered-off systems media and servers
- Examination and reporting

The full SWGDE best practices for computer forensics document can be downloaded from here:

```
https://www.swgde.org/documents/Current%20Documents/
SWGDE%20Best%20Practices%20for%20Computer%20Forensics
```

The *SWGDE Capture of Live Systems* document, version 2.0, released in September 2014, although quite short and not as detailed, is still applicable to forensic investigations involving live (powered-on) systems. This document provides guidelines when investigating live systems including the order of volatility, memory forensics including paging file forensics, and live physical and filesystem acquisition.

This document is only six pages long and can be downloaded from here:
```
https://www.swgde.org/documents/Current%20Documents/
SWGDE%20Capture%20of%20Live%20Systems
```

The **NIST (National Institute of Standards and Technology)** *Guidelines on Mobile Device Forensics* is also another very useful document that applies specifically to mobile devices. Revision one of this document, released in 2014, goes into great detail about the aspects of mobile forensics investigations. Its content includes:

- Mobile and cellular characteristics
- Evaluation and documentation of the scene
- Device isolation and packaging
- Device and memory acquisition
- Examination, analysis, and reporting

The full document can be downloaded here:

```
http://nvlpubs.nist.gov/nistpubs/SpecialPublications/NIST.SP.800-101r1.pdf
```

Summary

If there was one thing only that I'd like you to take away from this chapter, it would be to remember that the original evidence, particularly hard drives, storage media, and RAM images, should only used to create forensically-sound Bitstream copies. The original evidence is never to be worked on.

To recap, when a breach is reported, there should be an established first responder who, as per protocol, performs the tasks of documenting and securing the scene as well as collecting and preserving the evidence. The first responder should have a toolkit with various tools and items for the acquisition of evidence, and when handing over the evidence to other parties, ensure that the Chain of Custody is maintained.

We also had a look at the various procedures and best practices when investigating devices that are powered on and powered off, and also discussed the importance of using a write blocker to prevent the original evidence from being tampered with and then using a hashing tool for integrity verification purposes.

You've come this far, and I know it must have been a bit of an information overload, but now we can get to the practical section of this book where we can begin our investigation using digital forensics tools in Kali Linux. Let's go!

5
Evidence Acquisition and Preservation with DC3DD and Guymager

In the previous chapter, we learned that documentation and proper procedures are key in any investigation. These ensure the integrity of the investigation by providing proof of data authenticity and preservation of the original evidence and documentation, which can be used to achieve the same exact results if usage of tools and methods are repeated.

In this chapter, we will demonstrate forensically sound techniques for the acquisition of data using Bitstream copies inclusive of creating data hashes.

The first tool we will use for acquisition is called **DC3DD (Department of Defense Cyber Crime Center)**. DC3DD is a patch of the very popular Data Dump or DD tool, used for forensic acquisition and hashing.

These are the features of **Data Dump (DD)**:

- Bitstream (raw) disk acquisition and cloning
- Copying disk partitions
- Copying folders and files
- Hard disk drive error checking
- Forensic wiping of all data on hard disk drives

We will then explore another very popular acquisition tool called Guymager, which offers many of the same features in a GUI.

Drive and partition recognition in Linux

Users new to Kali or any Linux variations may find that the drive and partition recognition and naming in Kali are different to that of Windows devices.

A typical device in Linux can be addressed or recognized as /dev/sda, whereas drives in Windows are usually recognized as Disk 0 and Disk 1, and so on:

- /dev: Refers to the path of all devices and drives that can be read from or written to, recognized by Linux
- /sda: Refers to **SCSI (Small Computer Systems Interface)**, SATA, and USB devices

The **sd** stands for **SCSI Mass-Storage Driver**, with the letter after representing the drive number:

- sda: Drive 0 or the first drive recognized
- sdb: The second drive

While Windows recognizes partitions as primary, logical, and extended, Linux partitions are recognized as numbers, after the drive letter:

- sda1: Partition 1 on the first disk (sda)
- sda2: Partition 2 on the first disk
- sdb1: Partition 1 on the second disk (sdb)
- sdb2: Partition 2 on the second disk

Device identification using the fdisk command

Before we get started using DD, I need to again draw your attention to one of the features of DD, being the ability to wipe data, partitions, and drives. Hence, you may find that DD is sometimes also fondly referred to as the **Data Destroyer**. Be sure to always first identify your devices, partitions, input and output files, and parameters when using DD and DC3DD.

For the exercises in this chapter, I'll be using an old 2 GB flash drive for the acquisition process using DC3DD. To list your devices and ensure that you are aware of them before performing any acquisition operations, the fdisk -l command should be run before any other. The sudo fdisk -l command may have to be used if the previous one does not work.

In the following screenshot, the `fdisk -l` command has been run before attaching the 2 GB flash drive to list the devices already connected. There is one hard disk listed as `sda`. The Primary partition is listed as `sda1`, with the `Extended` and `Linux swap` partitions listed as `sda2` and `sda5`, respectively:

After attaching the 2 GB flash drive for acquisition, the `fdisk -l` command was run yet again and can be seen in the following screenshot with these details:

- **Disk**: `sdb`
- **Size**: `1.9 GB`
- **Sector size**: `512 bytes`
- **Filesystem**: `FAT32`

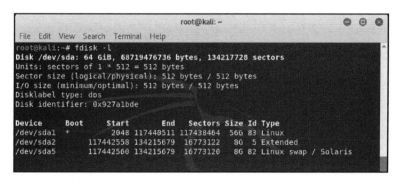

As seen in the previous screenshots (and also explained earlier in this chapter), Kali Linux recognizes two devices:

- sda: Primary hard disk with three partitions
- sdb: Flash drive to be forensically acquired or imaged

Now that we've distinguished and become certain of which drive is to be imaged (sdb) we can begin the forensic imaging using DC3DD.

 Although I have used an older 2 GB flash drive to demonstrate the usage of DC3DD, you can use any drive (portable or otherwise) to practice using the tools in this chapter. Be sure to use the fdisk -1 command to identify your drives and partitions.

Maintaining evidence integrity

In an effort to provide proof that the evidence was not tampered with, a hash of the evidence should be provided before and during, or after, an acquisition.

In Kali Linux, we can use the md5sum command followed by the path of the device, to create an MD5 hash of the evidence/input file. For example, md5sum /dev/sdx.

You may also try the command with superuser privileges by typing sudo md5sum /dev/sdx.

For this example, the 2 GB flash drive that I'll be using (named test_usb) is recognized as sdb, and so the command I will be using, is shown in the following screenshot:

```
root@kali:~# md5sum /dev/sdb
9f03801715e000c68cc319251301c7d3  /dev/sdb
```

In the previous example, the output of the md5sum of the 2 GB flash drive is displayed as 9f038....1c7d3 /dev/sdb. When performing the acquisition or forensic imaging of the drive using DC3DD, we should also have that exact result when hashing the created image file output to ensure that both the original evidence and the copy are exactly the same, thereby maintaining the integrity of the evidence.

I've also created an SHA-1 hash (which will be used for comparative purposes) using the following syntax:

```
root@kali:~# sha1sum /dev/sdb
0d5021a1abf889e4663b145f701b6e48e69e374a  /dev/sdb
```

Using DC3DD in Kali Linux

DC3DD was developed by the Department of Defense Cyber Crime Center and is updated whenever DD updates. DC3DD offers the best of DD with more features, including:

- On-the-fly hashing using more algorithm choices (MD5, SHA-1, SHA-256, and SHA-512)
- A meter to monitor progress and acquisition time
- Writing of errors to a file
- Splitting of output files
- Verification of files
- Wiping of output files (pattern wiping)

 Although we'll only be looking at DD and DC3DD, there is also another tool called **DCFLDD**, which can be installed on Linux-based systems. DCFLDD is an enhanced version of DD and is maintained and supported by the **Defense Computer Forensics Labs (DCFL)** with its own release schedule, unlike DC3DD which updates synchronized with DD.

DC3DD is a CLI and can be easily run in Kali Linux by first opening a Terminal and typing dc3dd. To start with, I recommend using the dc3dd --help command, which lists the available parameters used with dc3dd:

```
root@kali:~# dc3dd --help
------
usage:
------


        dc3dd [OPTION 1] [OPTION 2] ... [OPTION N]

                *or*

        dc3dd [HELP OPTION]

        where each OPTION is selected from the basic or advanced
        options listed below, or HELP OPTION is selected from the
        help options listed below.


--------------
basic options:
--------------

        if=DEVICE or FILE       Read input from a device or a file (see note #1
                                below for how to read from standard input). This
                                option can only be used once and cannot be
                                combined with ifs=, pat=, or tpat=.
        ifs=BASE.FMT            Read input from a set of files with base name
                                BASE and sequential file name extensions
                                conforming to the format specifier FMT (see note
                                #4 below for how to specify FMT). This option
                                can only be used once and cannot be combined with
                                if=, pat=, or tpat=.
        of=FILE or DEVICE       Write output to a file or device (see note #2
                                below for how to write to standard output). This
                                option can be used more than once (see note #3
                                below for how to generate multiple outputs).
        hof=FILE or DEVICE      Write output to a file or device, hash the
                                output bytes, and verify by comparing the output
                                hash(es) to the input hash(es). This option can
                                be used more than once (see note #3 below for
                                how to generate multiple outputs).
```

As seen in the previous screenshot using the dc3dd --help command, typical usage of the DC3DD command looks like this:

```
dc3dd [option 1] [option 2] ... [option n]
```

In our previous example, I've used the following options:

dc3dd if=/dev/sdb hash=md5 log=dc3ddusb of=test_usb.dd

```
root@kali:~# dc3dd if=/dev/sdb hash=md5 log=dc3ddusb of=test_usb.dd
```

- `if`: Specifies the *input file,* which is the device we will be imaging.
- `hash`: Specifies the type of hash algorithm we will be using for integrity verification. In this case, I have used the older MD5 hash.
- `log`: Specifies the name of the log file that logs the details of the device and the acquisition, including errors.
- `of`: Specifies the output file name of the forensic image created by DC3DD. Although a `.dd` image file type was specified in this example, other formats are recognized by DC3DD including `.img` as seen in a later example.

The device size (in sector and bytes) should be noted and later compared to the *output results for device* field.

The last line also displays the progress and status of the acquisition process, showing the amount of data copied, elapsed time in seconds, and the speed of the imaging process in Mbps:

```
root@kali:~# dc3dd if=/dev/sdb hash=md5 log=dc3ddusb of=test_usb.dd

dc3dd 7.2.646 started at 2017-11-03 06:23:25 -0400
compiled options:
command line: dc3dd if=/dev/sdb hash=md5 log=dc3ddusb of=test_usb.dd
device size: 3913664 sectors (probed),    2,003,795,968 bytes
sector size: 512 bytes (probed)
  1590591488 bytes ( 1.5 G ) copied ( 79% ),   97 s, 16 M/s
```

The larger the drive or file to be acquired, the lengthier the time taken to do so. Might I suggest you get yourself a cup of coffee or refreshing beverage, or even have a look at some other wonderful titles available from Packt at `https://www.packtpub.com/`.

Once the acquisition process has been completed, the input and output results are displayed:

```
  2003795968 bytes ( 1.9 G ) copied ( 100% ),  122 s, 16 M/s

input results for device `/dev/sdb':
   3913664 sectors in
   0 bad sectors replaced by zeros
   9f03801715e000c68cc319251301c7d3 (md5)

output results for file `test_usb.dd':
   3913664 sectors out

dc3dd completed at 2017-11-03 06:25:26 -0400

root@kali:~#
```

Analyzing the results, we can see that the same amount of sectors (3913664) have been imaged, with no bad sectors being replaced by zeros. We can also see that the exact MD5 hash was created for the image, assuring us that an exact copy was created without modification.

In the Terminal, we can also use the ls command to list the directory contents to ensure the DC3DD output file (test_usb.dd) and log (dc3ddusb) have been created:

To access our forensic image and log file, we can go to our /home directory by clicking on places (top left corner) and then Home.

Within my Home folder, the first file, 2GBdcedd.dd, is the output image created by DC3DD using the of=test_usb.dd command. The last file, dc3ddusb, is the log file, created when we used the log=dc3ddusb command:

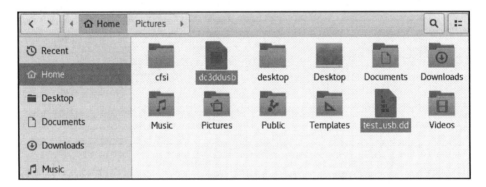

It's important to keep this log file to have a record of the acquisition process and its results, which were displayed on screen upon completion:

```
Open ▾  □                                    dc3ddusb

dc3dd 7.2.646 started at 2017-11-03 06:23:25 -0400
compiled options:
command line: dc3dd if=/dev/sdb hash=md5 log=dc3ddusb of=test_usb.dd
device size: 3913664 sectors (probed),    2,003,795,968 bytes
sector size: 512 bytes (probed)
  2003795968 bytes ( 1.9 G ) copied ( 100% ), 121.572 s, 16 M/s

input results for device `/dev/sdb':
   3913664 sectors in
   0 bad sectors replaced by zeros
   9f03801715e000c68cc319251301c7d3 (md5)

output results for file `test_usb.dd':
   3913664 sectors out

dc3dd completed at 2017-11-03 06:25:26 -0400
```

In future chapters, we will be analyzing acquired forensic images using various tools; however, the image can also be copied or directly cloned to another device if the investigator so wishes.

As an example, we could clone the forensic image acquired previously (test_usb.dd) onto a new drive recognized as sdc. The command used to perform this task would be:

```
dc3dd if=test_usb.dd of=/dev/sdc log=drivecopy.log
```

 When copying an image to a drive, the destination drive size should be of equal size or larger than the image file.

File-splitting using DC3DD

Depending on the size of the evidence, manageability and portability can become an issue. DC3DD has the ability to split forensically acquired images into multiple parts.

This is accomplished using the ofsz and ofs options:

- ofsz specifies the size of each output file part
- ofs specifies the output files with numerical file extensions, typically .000, .001, .002, and so on

Always ensure that you have specified enough zeros for the file extension. Logically, .000 allows for more parts than .00.

For this example, I've used the same 2 GB flash drive as before; however, for demonstrative purposes, you'll notice two changes.

Instead of using the MD5 hash, I've specified that SHA-1 be used and the output file type will be .img instead of the previously used .dd.

In this instance, the imaged 2 GB flash size will instead be split into multiple parts (four in total) of 500 MBs each using ofsz=500M with the parts named as 2GBdc3dd2.img.ooo, 2GBdc3dd2.img.oo1, 2GBdc3dd2.img.oo2, and 2GBdc3dd2.img.oo3.

The command used to achieve this is:

```
dc3dd if=/dev/sdb  hash=sha1  log=dd_split_usb  ofsz=500M
ofs=split_test_usb.img.ooo
```

```
root@kali:~# dc3dd if=/dev/sdb hash=sha1 log=dd_split_usb ofsz=500M ofs=split_test_usb.img.000

dc3dd 7.2.646 started at 2017-11-03 06:40:04 -0400
compiled options:
command line: dc3dd if=/dev/sdb hash=sha1 log=dd_split_usb ofsz=500M ofs=split_test_usb.img.000
device size: 3913664 sectors (probed),    2,003,795,968 bytes
sector size: 512 bytes (probed)
   369983488 bytes ( 353 M ) copied ( 18% ),    23 s, 16 M/s
```

Once completed, the input results for the device shows the SHA-1 hash output and also displays the first part of the split image files:

```
   2003795968 bytes ( 1.9 G ) copied ( 100% ),   123 s, 15 M/s

input results for device `/dev/sdb':
   3913664 sectors in
   0 bad sectors replaced by zeros
   0d5021a1abf889e4663b145f701b6e48e69e374a (sha1)

output results for files `split_test_usb.img.000':
   3913664 sectors out

dc3dd completed at 2017-11-03 06:42:07 -0400

root@kali:~#
```

Using the `ls` command once more, we can see that the extensions of each of the four split output files are all in numerical format from `.000` to `.003`:

```
root@kali:~# ls
cfsi          Desktop     Images    Public                 split_test_usb.img.002  Videos
dd_split_usb  Documents   Music     split_test_usb.img.000 split_test_usb.img.003
desktop       Downloads   Pictures  split_test_usb.img.001 Templates
root@kali:~#
```

All split parts of the imaged file can be found in the `Home` folder along with the log file:

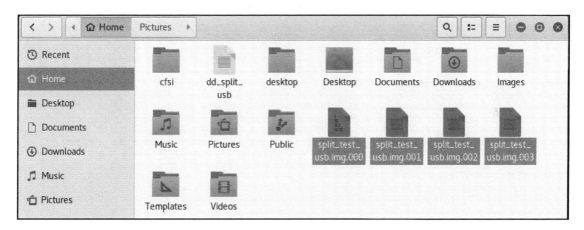

Verifying hashes of split image files

To verify the hash of the split files, the following command can be used:

```
cat split_test_usb.img.* | sha1sum
```

```
root@kali:~# cat split_test_usb.img.* | sha1sum
0d5021a1abf889e4663b145f701b6e48e69e374a  -
root@kali:~#
```

This also matches the `sha1sum` output of the 2 GB flash drive itself, displayed by using the following command:

```
sha1sum /dev/sdb
```

```
root@kali:~# sha1sum /dev/sdb
0d5021a1abf889e4663b145f701b6e48e69e374a  /dev/sdb
root@kali:~#
```

Erasing a drive using DC3DD

We've seen the power of DC3DD as a very impressive forensic acquisition tool, but I'd also like to go one step further and introduce you to its capabilities as a data wiping tool. DC3DD can wipe data and erase drives by overwriting data in three ways:

- Overwriting and filling the data and drives with zeroes. The command used is `dc3dd wipe=/dev/sdb`:

```
root@kali:~# dc3dd wipe=/dev/sdb

dc3dd 7.2.646 started at 2017-10-26 11:39:42 -0400
compiled options:
command line: dc3dd wipe=/dev/sdb
device size: 3913664 sectors (probed),    2,003,795,968 bytes
sector size: 512 bytes (probed)
  2003795968 bytes ( 1.9 G ) copied ( 100% ),   53 s, 36 M/s

input results for pattern `00':
   3913664 sectors in

output results for device `/dev/sdb':
   3913664 sectors out

dc3dd completed at 2017-10-26 11:40:34 -0400
```

- Overwriting and filling the data and drives using a hexadecimal pattern using the pat option. The command used is `dc3dd wipe=/dev/sdb pat=000111`:

```
root@kali:~# dc3dd wipe=/dev/sdb pat=000111

dc3dd 7.2.646 started at 2017-10-26 11:42:30 -0400
compiled options:
command line: dc3dd wipe=/dev/sdb pat=000111
device size: 3913664 sectors (probed),    2,003,795,968 bytes
sector size: 512 bytes (probed)
  2003795968 bytes ( 1.9 G ) copied ( 100% ),   165 s, 12 M/s

input results for pattern `000111':
   3913664 sectors in

output results for device `/dev/sdb':
   3913664 sectors out

dc3dd completed at 2017-10-26 11:45:16 -0400
```

- Overwriting and filling the data and drives using a text pattern using the `tpat` option. The command used is `dc3dd wipe=/dev/sdb tpat=cfsi:`

```
root@kali:~# dc3dd wipe=/dev/sdb tpat=cfsi

dc3dd 7.2.646 started at 2017-10-26 11:46:20 -0400
compiled options:
command line: dc3dd wipe=/dev/sdb tpat=cfsi
device size: 3913664 sectors (probed),    2,003,795,968 bytes
sector size: 512 bytes (probed)
  2003795968 bytes ( 1.9 G ) copied ( 100% ),  238 s, 8 M/s

input results for pattern `cfsi':
   3913664 sectors in

output results for device `/dev/sdb':
   3913664 sectors out

dc3dd completed at 2017-10-26 11:50:19 -0400
```

Image acquisition using Guymager

Guymager is another standalone acquisition tool that can be used for creating forensic images and also performing disk cloning. Developed by Guy Voncken, Guymager is completely open source, has many of the same features of DC3DD, and is also only available for Linux-based hosts. While some investigators may prefer CLI tools, Guymager is a GUI tool and it is for beginners, so it may be preferred.

For this acquisition, I'll also use the very same 2 GB flash drive used in the DC3DD examples, at the end of which we can compare results. It's also important to remember to continue using your write-blocker when acquiring and creating forensic images of evidence and drives, in an effort to not write data to the drives or modify the original evidence files.

As previously done in the DC3DD acquisition, we should first ensure that we are familiar with the devices attached to our machine, using the `fdisk -l` or `sudo fdisk -l` command.

Running Guymager

Guymager can be started by using the menu in Kali and by clicking on **Applications** on the side menu, and then click on **Forensics** and scroll down to **Guymager**:

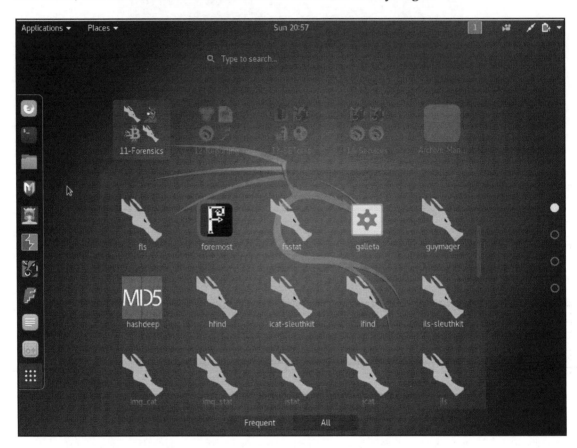

Guymager can also be started using the Terminal by typing `guymager`. You may also try the `sudo guymager` command. Once started, the default locations of the log file and configuration (`cfg`) files, which can be changed if required:

```
File  Edit  View  Search  Terminal  Help
root@kali:~# guymager

Using default log file name /var/log/guymager.log
Using default cfg file name /etc/guymager/guymager.cfg

Help
```

The Guymager application runs and then displays the existing drives recognized in Kali Linux. As seen in the following screenshot, the details of the 2 GB flash drive being used are shown, including the following:

- **Linux device**: Recognized as /dev/sdb
- **Model**: USB_Flash_Memory
- **State**: Shown as **Idle** as the image acquisition has not yet begun
- **Size**: 2.0GB

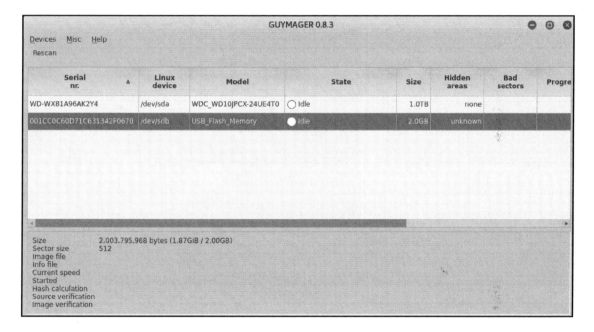

Should your device not be listed in Guymager or should you need to add an additional device, click the **Rescan** button at the top-left corner of the application.

Acquiring evidence with Guymager

To begin the acquisition process, right-click on the evidence drive (/dev/sdb in this example) and select **Acquire image**. Note that the **Clone device** option is also available should you wish to clone the evidence drive to another. Again, as previously mentioned, when cloning a device, the capacity of the destination device must be equal to or exceed that of the source (original) evidence drive:

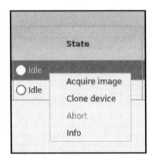

Before the actual acquisition process starts, the investigator is prompted to enter details about themselves and the evidence under the following three sections:

- **File format**:
  - **File extensions**: .dd, .xxx, and .Exx
  - **Split size**: Allows the investigator to choose the size of multiple image parts
  - **Case management information**: **Case number**, **Evidence number**, **Examiner** name, **Description**, and **Notes**

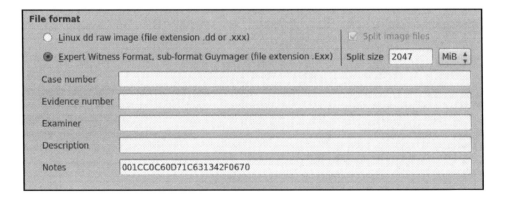

- **Destination**:
  - **Image directory**: The location of the created image file and log (info file)
  - **Image filename**: The name of the image file

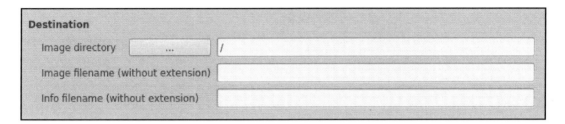

- **Hash calculation / verification**:
  - Multiple hashing algorithms can be selected and calculated, allowing the investigator to choose from MD5, SHA-1, and SHA256
  - **Re-read source after acquisition for verification**: This verifies the source
  - **Verify image after acquisition**: This verifies the destination

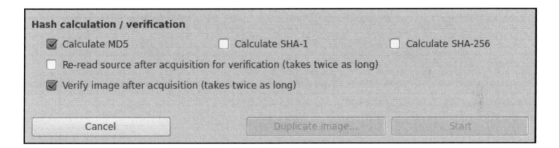

Guymager also adds the convenience of having a **Duplicate image...** button to create duplicate copies without having to repeat the the data entry process.

For new users, you may want to specify the directory where the image file will be saved. In the destination section, click on the **Image directory** button and choose your location. For this acquisition, I've chosen the Desktop directory as the location for both the image and the log/info file:

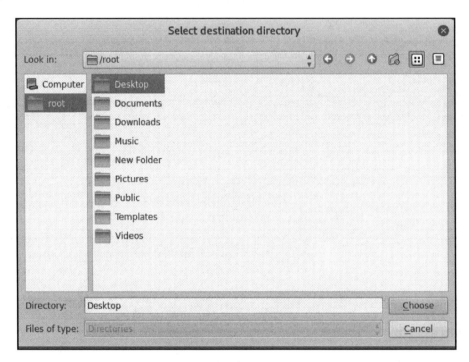

The following screenshot shows the data that I've used for the Guymager acquisition, having chosen the Desktop as the **Image directory** and MD5 and SHA-1 hashing algorithms:

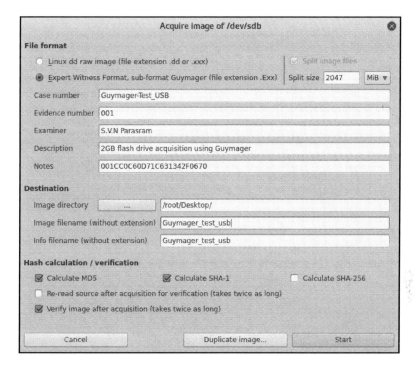

Once the **Start** button is clicked, you will notice that the **State** changes from **Idle** to **Running**. The **Progress** field also now displays a progress bar:

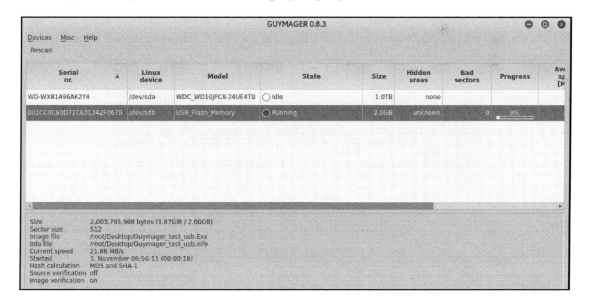

Taking a closer look at the details on the lower left corner of the screen, we see the size, image, and info file paths, names and extensions, current speed, and chosen hash calculations. We also see that **Image verification** is turned **on**:

```
Size                  2,003,795,968 bytes (1.87GiB / 2.00GB)
Sector size           512
Image file            /root/Desktop/Guymager_test_usb.Exx
Info file             /root/Desktop/Guymager_test_usb.info
Current speed         21.94 MB/s
Started               3. November 06:56:11 (00:00:40)
Hash calculation      MD5 and SHA-1
Source verification   off
Image verification    on
```

Once the acquisition process is completed, the color of the **State** field button changes from blue to green, indicating that the acquisition process is finished, and it also displays **Finished - Verified & ok**, if verification options were selected in the Hash verification/calculation area. The progress bar also displays **100%**:

Serial nr.	▲	Linux device	Model	State	Size	Hidden areas	Bad sectors	Progress
001CC0C60D71C631342F0670		/dev/sdb	USB_Flash_Memory	● Finished - Verified & ok	2.0GB	unknown	0	100%
VB2aae48a1-1ad25067		/dev/sda	VBOX_HARDDISK	○ Idle	34.4GB	unknown		

Our output file and info file can be found on the `Desktop` as this was specified in the **Acquire images** section earlier. If you have selected a different directory, change to the new directory using the `cd` command, in a new Terminal. In the following screenshot, I've changed to the `Desktop` directory using the `cd Desktop` command and then listed the contents using the `ls` command:

```
root@kali:~#
root@kali:~# cd Desktop
root@kali:~/Desktop# ls
CFSI  Guymager_test_usb.E01  Guymager_test_usb.info
root@kali:~/Desktop#
root@kali:~/Desktop#
```

We can also browse the `Desktop`, or even the `Desktop` folder, to open the info file, which presents us with information about the acquisition details:

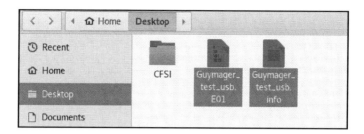

Hash verification

Double-clicking on the info file in the **Image directory** location allows us to inspect a variety of details about the acquisition process from start to completion, including the hashed outputs.

This info file contains much more data than the log file produced by DC3DD, including the case management details:

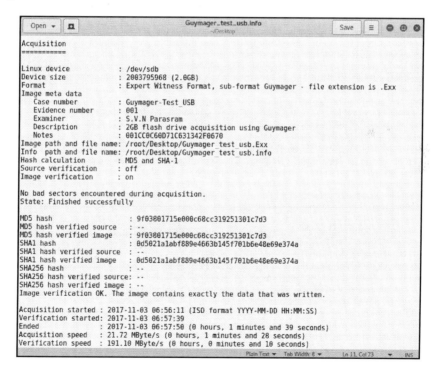

Let's have a closer look at the hash details within the `.info` file.

We can see that the MD5 and SHA-1 hashes have been created and verified and, as stated in the last line of the following screenshot, `Image verification OK. The image contains exactly the data that was written`:

```
MD5 hash                    : 9f03801715e000c68cc319251301c7d3
MD5 hash verified source    : --
MD5 hash verified image     : 9f03801715e000c68cc319251301c7d3
SHA1 hash                   : 0d5021a1abf889e4663b145f701b6e48e69e374a
SHA1 hash verified source   : --
SHA1 hash verified image    : 0d5021a1abf889e4663b145f701b6e48e69e374a
SHA256 hash                 : --
SHA256 hash verified source : --
SHA256 hash verified image  : --
Image verification OK. The image contains exactly the data that was written.
```

If we compare these hashes with the ones created using DC3DD, we would have the exact same MD5 and SHA-1 outputs, proving that these images are exact forensic copies of the original evidence.

Compare the hashes in the following screenshots, created by DC3DD, with the ones in the previous screenshots, created by Guymager:

- **DC3DD MD5 Hash**:

```
   9f03801715e000c68cc319251301c7d3 (md5)

output results for file `test_usb.dd':
    3913664 sectors out
```

- **DC3DD SHA-1 Hash**:

```
   0d5021a1abf889e4663b145f701b6e48e69e374a (sha1)

output results for files `split_test_usb.img.000':
    3913664 sectors out

dc3dd completed at 2017-11-03 06:42:07 -0400
```

Summary

In this chapter, we've looked at two tools readily available in Kali Linux for the acquisition of digital evidence. It's very important to be able to tell your devices apart so you can accurately acquire a forensic and exact copy or image of the evidence file using the `fdisk - l` command. For forensic analysis, Bitstream copies of the evidence are needed as these provide an exact copy of the evidence, bit-by-bit, which is why we used DC3DD and Guymager.

Firstly, we used DC3DD, the enhancement of the data dump tool, and through the Terminal, performed quite a few tasks including device imaging, hashing, splitting of files, and file verification. Although DC3DD is a command-line interface program, the options remain the same, making it fairly easy to learn and use.

Our second tool, Guymager, has built-in case-management abilities and also has many functional similarities to DC3DD, but it comes as a GUI tool and may be easier to use.

Both tools deliver accurate and forensically sound results. For those that may not be constantly working with Guymager, DD, and DC3DD, Guymager may be the easier tool to use seeing that all acquisition options including cloning are readily available through the GUI, along with an easy to read log, which provides case management details. For advanced uses such as drive wiping, however, you may wish to use DC3DD. In the end, however, the choice remains yours.

Not bad for our first forensics tools in Kali Linux. Next, we'll move on to some analysis and file recovery tools using actual forensic images created by **NIST** (**National Institute of Standards and Technology**). Exciting stuff!

6

File Recovery and Data Carving with Foremost, Scalpel, and Bulk Extractor

Now that we've learned how to create forensic images of evidence, let's take a look at the file recovery and data carving process using Foremost, Scalpel, and Bulk Extractor.

When we last covered filesystems, we saw that various operating systems use their own filesystems to be able to store, access, and modify data. So too, storage media use filesystems to do the very same.

Metadata, or data about data, helps the operating system identify the data. Metadata includes technical information, such as the creation and modification dates, and the file type of the data. This data makes it much easier to locate and index files.

File carving retrieves data and files from unallocated space using specific characteristics such as file structure and file headers, instead of traditional metadata created by, or associated with, filesystems.

As the name implies, **unallocated space** is an area of storage media that has been marked by the operating system or file table as empty or unallocated to any file or data. Although the location of, and information about, the files are not present and sometimes corrupted, there are still characteristics about the file that reside in its header and footer that can identify the file or even fragments of the file.

Even if a file extension has been changed or is missing altogether, file headers contain information that can identify the file type and attempt to carve the file by analyzing header and footer information. Data carving is quite a lengthy process and should be done using automated tools to save time. It also helps if the investigator has an idea of what file types they are looking for, to have a better focus and to save time. Nevertheless, this is forensics and we know that time and patience are key.

Some common file types, as displayed in hexadecimal format within the file headers, include:

- **Joint Photographic Experts Group (JPEG)**: FF D8 FF E0
- **Portable Document Format (PDF)**: 25 50 44 46

While more on analysis of files and headers will be looked at in later chapters, let's have a look at three tools for data carving in Kali Linux.

Forensic test images used in Foremost and Scalpel

For this tool, a digital forensic tool testing image, created by Nick Micus, specifically for testing data carving tools, was used. One of the main reasons for choosing this particular image for this exercise is that Nick Mikus is listed as one of the contributing developers of Foremost. As seen in the first line of Foremost, which displays the version number alongside authors Jesse Kornblum and Kris Kendall. The image can be downloaded freely at http://dftt.sourceforge.net/test11/index.html.

Once you've become familiar with this exercise, you can try extracting data from other images also available on that site at http://dftt.sourceforge.net/.

Using Foremost for file recovery and data carving

Foremost is a simple and effective CLI tool that recovers files by reading the headers and footers of the files. We can start Foremost by clicking on **Applications** | **11-Forensics** | **foremost**:

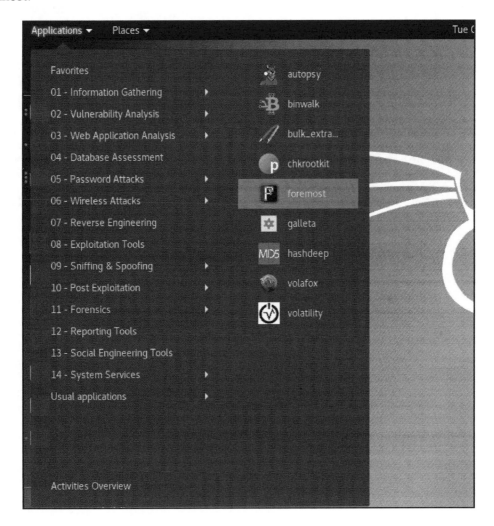

Once Foremost is successfully started, a Terminal opens, displaying the program version, creators, and some of the many switches for usage:

```
                              root@kali: ~                        ⊖  ⊙  ⊗
 File  Edit  View  Search  Terminal  Help
foremost version 1.5.7 by Jesse Kornblum, Kris Kendall, and Nick Mikus.
$ foremost [-v|-V|-h|-T|-Q|-q|-a|-w-d] [-t <type>] [-s <blocks>] [-k <size>]
          [-b <size>] [-c <file>] [-o <dir>] [-i <file]

-V  - display copyright information and exit
-t  - specify file type.  (-t jpeg,pdf ...)
-d  - turn on indirect block detection (for UNIX file-systems)
-i  - specify input file (default is stdin)
-a  - Write all headers, perform no error detection (corrupted files)
-w  - Only write the audit file, do not write any detected files to the disk
-o  - set output directory (defaults to output)
-c  - set configuration file to use (defaults to foremost.conf)
-q  - enables quick mode. Search are performed on 512 byte boundaries.
-Q  - enables quiet mode. Suppress output messages.
-v  - verbose mode. Logs all messages to screen
root@kali:~# █
```

To have a better understanding of Foremost and the switches used, try browsing the Foremost System Manager's Manual. This can be done by entering the following command:

```
man foremost
```

```
FOREMOST(8)                  System Manager's Manual                  FOREMOST(8)

NAME
       foremost  - Recover files using their headers, footers, and data struc-
       tures

SYNOPSIS
       foremost [-h] [-V] [-d] [-vqwQT] [-b <blocksize>] [-o <dir>] [-t
       <type>] [-s <num>] [-i <file>]

BUILTIN FORMATS
       Recover  files  from  a disk image based on file types specified by the
       user using the -t switch.

       jpg     Support for the JFIF and Exif formats including  implementations
               used in modern digital cameras.

       gif

       png

       bmp     Support for windows bmp format.

       avi

       exe     Support  for Windows PE binaries, will extract DLL and EXE files
               along with their compile times.

       mpg     Support for most MPEG files (must begin with 0x000001BA)
```

The syntax for using Foremost is as follows:

```
foremost -i (forensic image) -o (output folder) -options
```

In this example, we have specified the `11-carve-fat.dd` file located on the desktop as the input file (`-i`) and specified an empty folder named `Foremost_recovery` as the output file (`-o`). Additionally, other switches can also be specified as needed.

To begin carving the `11-carve-fat.dd` image with Foremost, we type the following command in the Terminal:

```
foremost -i 11-carve-fat.dd -o Foremost_recovery
```

Although the characters found look quite unclear while processing, the results will be clearly categorized and summarized in the specified output folder.

For quick access to some of the commands in Foremost, you may also use `foremost -h`.

It is important that the specified output folder be empty or you will encounter problems, as shown in the following screenshot:

```
Foremost started at Tue Oct 24 08:33:20 2017
Invocation: foremost -i/root/Desktop/Graphic.dd -o/root/Desktop/Recovered -v
Output directory: /root/Desktop/Recovered
Configuration file: /etc/foremost.conf
Processing: stdin
|-------------------------------------------------------------------
File: stdin
Start: Tue Oct 24 08:33:20 2017
Length: Unknown

Num     Name (bs=512)        Size        File Offset      Comment
```

Viewing Foremost results

Once Foremost has completed the carving process, we can proceed to the
`Foremost_recovery` output folder:

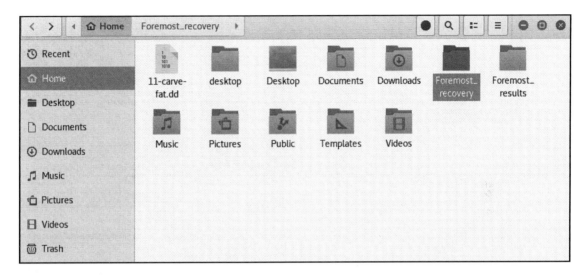

If we open the output directory, we can see the carved items, categorized by file type along
with an `audit.txt` folder, which contains details of the findings:

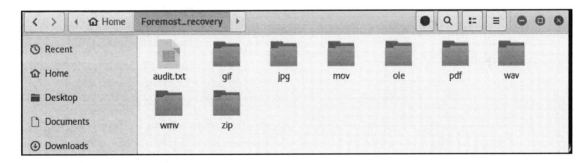

Within the `audit.text` file, we see a list view of the items found by Foremost, along with their `Sizes` and `File Offset` location:

```
Open  ▾   ⬛                          audit.txt                              Save
                                 ~/Foremost_recovery

Foremost version 1.5.7 by Jesse Kornblum, Kris Kendall, and Nick Mikus
Audit File

Foremost started at Tue Oct 24 11:05:17 2017
Invocation: foremost -i 11-carve-fat.dd -o Foremost_recovery
Output directory: /root/Foremost_recovery
Configuration file: /etc/foremost.conf
------------------------------------------------------------------
File: 11-carve-fat.dd
Start: Tue Oct 24 11:05:17 2017
Length: 61 MB (64979456 bytes)

Num      Name (bs=512)        Size      File Offset    Comment

0:       00019717.jpg        29 KB       10095104
1:       00019777.jpg       433 KB       10125824
2:       00020645.jpg        96 KB       10570240
3:       00020841.gif         5 KB       10670592      (88 x 31)
4:       00000321.wmv         7 MB         164352
5:       00021929.wmv      1012 KB       11227648
6:       00020853.mov       537 KB       10676736
7:       00016021.wav       311 KB        8202752
8:       00000281.ole        20 KB         143872
9:       00016693.ole        24 KB        8546816
10:      00023957.ole         6 MB       12265984
11:      00023981.zip        77 KB       12278272
12:      00016741.pdf         1 MB        8571392      (PDF is Linearized)
13:      00019477.pdf       119 KB        9972224
Finish: Tue Oct 24 11:05:18 2017
```

When scrolling down on the `audit.txt` file, you should see a summary of the files found, which is particularly useful when carving larger images:

```
14 FILES EXTRACTED

jpg:= 3
gif:= 1
wmv:= 2
mov:= 1
rif:= 1
ole:= 3
zip:= 1
pdf:= 2
------------------------------------------------------------------

Foremost finished at Tue Oct 24 11:05:18 2017
```

The first three files listed in the `audit.txt` files are `.jpg` image files and we can see these files in the `jpg` sub-folder within the `Foremost_recovery` output folder:

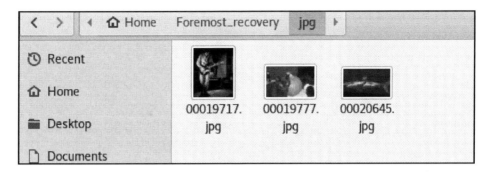

As we can see, Foremost is quite the powerful data recovery and file carving tool. File carving can take a very long time depending on the size of the drive or image used. If the type of file that needs to be recovered is already known, it may be wise to specify this type of file using the `-t` option, to reduce the amount of time taken when compared with searching the entire image.

Before running Foremost again, remember to choose a new or empty output folder.

Using Scalpel for data carving

Scalpel was created as an improvement of a much earlier version of Foremost. Scalpel aims to address the high CPU and RAM usage issues of Foremost when carving data.

Specifying file types in Scalpel

Unlike Foremost, file types of interest must be specified by the investigator in the Scalpel configuration file. This file is called `scalpel.conf` and is located at `etc/scapel/`:

To specify the file types, the investigator must remove the comments at the start of the line containing the file type as all supported file types are commented out with a hashtag at the beginning of the file type. The following screenshot shows the default Scalpel configuration file (`scalpel.conf`) with all file types commented out. Notice that each line begins with a hashtag:

```
#
# GIF and JPG files (very common)
#       gif     y       5000000         \x47\x49\x46\x38\x37\x61             \x00\x3b
#       gif     y       5000000         \x47\x49\x46\x38\x39\x61             \x00\x3b
#       jpg     y       200000000       \xff\xd8\xff\xe0\x00\x10             \xff\xd9
#
#
# PNG
#       png     y       20000000        \x50\x4e\x47?    \xff\xfc\xfd\xfe
#
#
# BMP     (used by MSWindows, use only if you have reason to think there are
#         BMP files worth digging for. This often kicks back a lot of false
#         positives
#
#       bmp     y       100000  BM??\x00\x00\x00
#
# TIFF
#       tif     y       200000000       \x49\x49\x2a\x00
# TIFF
#       tif     y       200000000       \x4D\x4D\x00\x2A
#
#
```

We've removed the hash tags at the beginning of some of the lines to let Scalpel know to search for these specific file types, this also reduces the time taken to otherwise search for all supported file types. The following screenshot shows that Scalpel will be searching for GIF and JPG files as the comments have been removed:

```
#
# GIF and JPG files (very common)
          gif     y      5000000      \x47\x49\x46\x38\x37\x61      \x00\x3b
          gif     y      5000000      \x47\x49\x46\x38\x39\x61      \x00\x3b
          jpg     y      200000000    \xff\xd8\xff\xe0\x00\x10      \xff\xd9
#
#
# PNG
          png     y      20000000     \x50\x4e\x47?   \xff\xfc\xfd\xfe
#
#
# BMP    (used by MSWindows, use only if you have reason to think there are
#         BMP files worth digging for. This often kicks back a lot of false
#         positives
#
|         bmp     y      100000  BM??\x00\x00\x00
#
# TIFF
#         tif     y      200000000    \x49\x49\x2a\x00
# TIFF
#         tif     y      200000000    \x4D\x4D\x00\x2A
#
```

Be sure to perform this step before specifying the image to be carved. Failure to do so presents the investigator with a helpful error message reminding them to do so.

```
ERROR: The configuration file didn't specify any file types to carve.
(If you're using the default configuration file, you'll have to
uncomment some of the file types.)

See /etc/scalpel/scalpel.conf.
root@kali:~#
```

Using Scalpel for file carving

Once we have made our changes to include file types and saved the `scalpel.conf` file, we can then start Scalpel by clicking on the Show Applications button on the sidebar and enter `scalpel` into the search box which then appears at the top of the screen, as seen here. Click on the `scalpel` box to begin:

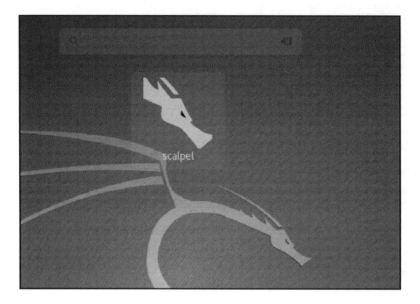

Once started, a Terminal opens showing the version number (1.60), the author (Golden G. Richard III), and as mentioned, states that it is based on Foremost 0.69. As seen with Foremost, Scalpel-usage syntax and additional options are also displayed:

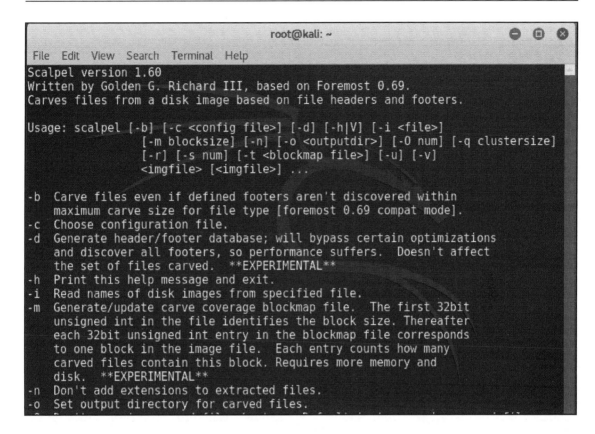

Scalpel version 1.60
Written by Golden G. Richard III, based on Foremost 0.69.
Carves files from a disk image based on file headers and footers.

Usage: scalpel [-b] [-c <config file>] [-d] [-h|V] [-i <file>]
                [-m blocksize] [-n] [-o <outputdir>] [-O num] [-q clustersize]
                [-r] [-s num] [-t <blockmap file>] [-u] [-v]
                <imgfile> [<imgfile>] ...

-b Carve files even if defined footers aren't discovered within
    maximum carve size for file type [foremost 0.69 compat mode].
-c Choose configuration file.
-d Generate header/footer database; will bypass certain optimizations
    and discover all footers, so performance suffers. Doesn't affect
    the set of files carved. **EXPERIMENTAL**
-h Print this help message and exit.
-i Read names of disk images from specified file.
-m Generate/update carve coverage blockmap file. The first 32bit
    unsigned int in the file identifies the block size. Thereafter
    each 32bit unsigned int entry in the blockmap file corresponds
    to one block in the image file. Each entry counts how many
    carved files contain this block. Requires more memory and
    disk. **EXPERIMENTAL**
-n Don't add extensions to extracted files.
-o Set output directory for carved files.

For this example, the same image used for carving with Foremost (`11-carve-fat.dd`) was used. As with Foremost also, the input file and output folder must be specified. To list the available options and switches in Scalpel, use `scalpel -h`.

The following syntax was used in Scalpel:

```
scalpel -o scalpelOutput/ 11-carve-fat.dd
```

```
root@kali:~# scalpel -o scalpelOutput/ 11-carve-fat.dd
Scalpel version 1.60
Written by Golden G. Richard III, based on Foremost 0.69.

Opening target "/root/11-carve-fat.dd"

Image file pass 1/2.
11-carve-fat.dd: 100.0% |*****************************|   62.0 MB    00:00 ETAAllocating work queues...
Work queues allocation complete. Building carve lists...
Carve lists built.  Workload:
gif with header "\x47\x49\x46\x38\x39\x61" and footer "\x00\x3b" --> 1 files
jpg with header "\xff\xd8\xff\xe0\x00\x10" and footer "\xff\xd9" --> 5 files
mov with header "\x3f\x3f\x3f\x3f\x6d\x6f\x6f\x76" and footer "" --> 1 files
mov with header "\x3f\x3f\x3f\x3f\x6d\x64\x61\x74" and footer "" --> 2 files
mov with header "\x3f\x3f\x3f\x3f\x77\x69\x64\x65\x76\x76" and footer "" --> 0 files
mpg with header "\x00\x00\x01\xba" and footer "\x00\x00\x01\xb9" --> 0 files
mpg with header "\x00\x00\x01\xb3" and footer "\x00\x00\x01\xb7" --> 0 files
doc with header "\xd0\xcf\x11\xe0\xa1\xb1\x1a\xe1\x00\x00" and footer "\xd0\xcf\x11\xe0\xa1\xb1\x1a\xe1\x00\x00" --> 3 files
doc with header "\xd0\xcf\x11\xe0\xa1\xb1" and footer "" --> 3 files
pst with header "\x21\x42\x4e\xa5\x6f\xb5\xa6" and footer "" --> 0 files
ost with header "\x21\x42\x44\x4e" and footer "" --> 0 files
dbx with header "\xcf\xad\x12\xfe\xc5\xfd\x74\x6f" and footer "" --> 0 files
idx with header "\x4a\x4d\x46\x39" and footer "" --> 0 files
mbx with header "\x4a\x4d\x46\x36" and footer "" --> 0 files
htm with header "\x3c\x68\x74\x6d\x6c" and footer "\x3c\x2f\x68\x74\x6d\x6c\x3e" --> 0 files
pdf with header "\x25\x50\x44\x46" and footer "\x25\x45\x4f\x46\x0d" --> 1 files
pdf with header "\x25\x50\x44\x46" and footer "\x25\x45\x4f\x46\x0a" --> 2 files
zip with header "\x50\x4b\x03\x04" and footer "\x3c\xac" --> 0 files
Carving files from image.
Image file pass 2/2.
11-carve-fat.dd: 100.0% |*****************************|   62.0 MB    00:00 ETAProcessing of image file complete. Cleaning up...
Done.
Scalpel is done, files carved = 18, elapsed = 2 seconds.
root@kali:~#
```

In the previous screenshot, we can see that Scalpel builds a carve-list showing the file type with header and footer information as well as the number of files carved.

Taking a closer look at the last few lines produced by the Scalpel output, we can see that the carving process was `100%` complete with `18` files being carved:

```
11-carve-fat.dd: 100.0% |*****************************|   62.0 MB    00:00 ETA
Processing of image file complete. Cleaning up...
Done.
Scalpel is done, files carved = 18, elapsed = 2 seconds.
root@kali:~#
```

Viewing results of Scalpel

Now we can head over to the output folder named `ScalpelOutput` to have a look at the carved files:

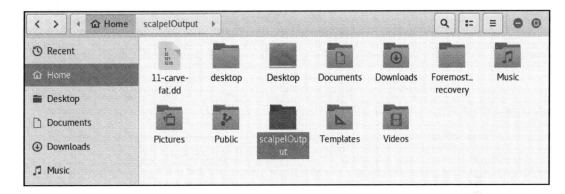

The results of the Scalpel output are similar to that of Foremost, with both output folders containing various subfolders with carved files along with an `audit.txt` file with details of the findings:

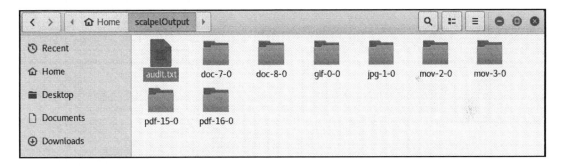

Within the `jpg-1-o` folder, we can see five `.jpg` files, three with actual images:

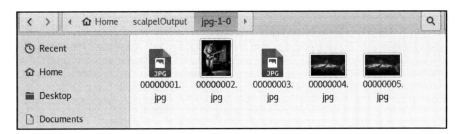

Even though Scalpel's results showed that five files with .jpg headers and footers were identified in the carve list when the tool was run, some of these may not open. These files are most likely false positives:

```
Carve lists built.  Workload:
gif with header "\x47\x49\x46\x38\x39\x61" and footer "\x00\x3b" --> 1 files
jpg with header "\xff\xd8\xff\xe0\x00\x10" and footer "\xff\xd9" --> 5 files
mov with header "\x3f\x3f\x3f\x3f\x6d\x6f\x6f\x76" and footer "" --> 1 files
mov with header "\x3f\x3f\x3f\x3f\x6d\x64\x61\x74" and footer "" --> 2 files
```

The following screenshot shows a snippet of the audit.txt file, displaying information about the carved files:

```
                                          audit.txt
 Open  ▼    ⟂                            ~/scalpelOutput               Save    ≡

Scalpel version 1.60 audit file
Started at Wed Oct 25 12:03:15 2017
Command line:
scalpel -o scalpelOutput/ 11-carve-fat.dd

Output directory: /root/scalpelOutput
Configuration file: /etc/scalpel/scalpel.conf

Opening target "/root/11-carve-fat.dd"

The following files were carved:
File            Start       Chop      Length       Extracted From
00000009.doc    143872      NO        8402944      11-carve-fat.dd
00000002.jpg    10095104    NO        29885        11-carve-fat.dd
00000001.jpg    8522240     NO        24367        11-carve-fat.dd
00000012.doc    143872      YES       10000000     11-carve-fat.dd
00000015.pdf    8571392     NO        1399508      11-carve-fat.dd
00000016.pdf    8571392     NO        1523266      11-carve-fat.dd
00000017.pdf    9972224     NO        122434       11-carve-fat.dd
00000010.doc    8546816     NO        3719168      11-carve-fat.dd
00000013.doc    8546816     YES       10000000     11-carve-fat.dd
00000008.mov    10678017    YES       10000000     11-carve-fat.dd
00000007.mov    10678001    YES       10000000     11-carve-fat.dd
00000006.mov    10676736    YES       10000000     11-carve-fat.dd
00000005.jpg    10574693    NO        2655         11-carve-fat.dd
00000004.jpg    10570636    NO        2655         11-carve-fat.dd
00000003.jpg    10570240    NO        3051         11-carve-fat.dd
00000000.gif    10670592    NO        5498         11-carve-fat.dd
00000014.doc    12265984    YES       10000000     11-carve-fat.dd
00000011.doc    12265984    NO        10000000     11-carve-fat.dd


Completed at Wed Oct 25 12:03:17 2017
```

Comparing Foremost and Scalpel

Although Scalpel returned more files than Foremost, carry out your own exercise in comparing the carved files found by both Foremost and Scalpel. Unfortunately, the filenames returned by both tools are not the original filenames and in some instances, there may be duplicates of carved files as many files may be fragmented and appear to be separate files. Try manually going through the files found in the output folders of both Foremost and Scalpel and do your own comparative research to see which tool was more successful.

The test image file (`11-carve-fat.dd`) used in both Foremost and Scalpel contains 15 files of various types, as listed on the download page (`http://dftt.sourceforge.net/test11/index.html`). This should be useful when doing a comparison of the carved files:

Num	Name	MD5	Size	Note	Sectors
1	2003_document.doc	e72f388b36f9370f19696b164c308482	19968	A Valid DOC file	(0-38) 281 -320
2	enterprise.wav	7629b89adade055f6783dc1773274215	318895	A valid WAV file	(0-622) 16021 -16644
3	haxor2.jpg	84e1dceac2eb127fef5bfdcb0eae324b	24367	An invalid JPEG with only 1 header byte corrupted. This byte is located at offset 19 within the file.	(0-47)16645 -16692
4	holly.xls	7917baf0219645afef8b381570c41211	23040	A valid XLS file	(0-44) 16693-16738
5	lin_1.2.pdf	e026ec863410725ba1f5765a1874800d	1399508	A linearized PDF	(0-2733) 16741 -19475
6	nlin_14.pdf	5b3e806e8c9c06a475cd45bf821af709	122434	A non-linearized PDF	(0-239) 19477 -19716
7	paul.jpg	37a49f97ed279832cd4f7bd002c826a2	29885	A valid jpeg	(0-58) 19717 -19776
8	pumpkin.jpg	6c9859e5121ff54d5d6298f65f0bf3b3	444314	A valid EXIF jpeg	(0-867) 19777-20644
9	shark.jpg	d83428b8742a075b57b0dc424cd297c4	99298	A valid JPEG	(0-193) 20645-20839
10	sm1.gif	d25fb845e6a41395adaed8bd14db7bf2	5498	A valid GIF	(0-10) 20841-20852
11	surf.mov	5328d2b066f428ea95b2793849ab97fa	550653	A valid MOV	(0-1075) 20853-21928
12	surf.wmv	ff085d0c4d0e0fdc8f3427db68e26266	1036994	A valid WMV	(0-2025) 21929-23955
13	test.ppt	7b74c2c608d92f4bb76c1d3b6bd1decc	11264	A deleted PPT	(0-21) 23957 -23978
14	wword60t.zip	c0be59d49b7ee0fdc492d2df32f2c6c6	78899	A valid ZIP	(0-154) 23981 -24135
15	domopers.wmv	63c0c6986cf0a446cb54b0ac65a921a5	8037267	A deleted wmv	(0-15697) 321-16018

Bulk_extractor

Bulk_extractor is the third and final tool that we'll cover in this chapter. Foremost and Scalpel, as we've seen so far, are quite impressive at file recovery and carving, but are limited to specific file types. For further extraction of data, we can use Bulk Extractor.

While Foremost and Scalpel can recover images, audio, video, and compressed files, Bulk Extractor extracts several additional types of information that can be very useful in investigations.

Although Bulk Extractor is quite capable of recovering and carving image, video, and document type files, other data that can be carved and extracted by Bulk Extractor includes:

- Credit card numbers
- Email addresses
- URLs
- Online searches
- Website information
- Social media profiles and information

Forensic test image for Bulk_extractor

For this example, we will work with a freely-available evidence file named `terry-work-usb-2009-12-11.E01`.

This file can be downloaded directly from the digital corpora website which allows the use of forensic evidence images for forensic research purposes. The file used in this exercise can be downloaded directly from `http://downloads.digitalcorpora.org/corpora/scenarios/2009-m57-patents/drives-redacted/`.

The required file is the last file on the download page and is only 32 MB in size:

Using Bulk_extractor

Start Bulk Extractor by first typing `bulk_extractor -h` to display some commonly-used parameters and options:

```
root@kali:~# bulk_extractor -h
bulk_extractor version 1.6.0-dev
Usage: bulk_extractor [options] imagefile
  runs bulk_extractor and outputs to stdout a summary of what was found where

Required parameters:
   imagefile       - the file to extract
  or  -R filedir  - recurse through a directory of files
                    HAS SUPPORT FOR E01 FILES
                    HAS SUPPORT FOR AFF FILES
  -o outdir       - specifies output directory. Must not exist.
                    bulk_extractor creates this directory.
Options:
  -i              - INFO mode. Do a quick random sample and print a report.
  -b banner.txt- Add banner.txt contents to the top of every output file.
  -r alert_list.txt  - a file containing the alert list of features to alert
                    (can be a feature file or a list of globs)
                    (can be repeated.)
  -w stop_list.txt   - a file containing the stop list of features (white list
                    (can be a feature file or a list of globs)s
                    (can be repeated.)
  -F <rfile>    - Read a list of regular expressions from <rfile> to find
  -f <regex>    - find occurrences of <regex>; may be repeated.
                    results go into find.txt
  -q nn          - Quiet Rate; only print every nn status reports. Default 0; -1
for no status at all
  -s frac[:passes] - Set random sampling parameters
```

Like Foremost and Scalpel, the syntax for using bulk_extractor is quite simple and requires that an output folder (-o) and the forensic image be specified. For this exercise, as previously mentioned, we will be extracting data from the terry-work-usb-2009-12-11.E01 image and saving the output to a folder named bulk-output.

The syntax used is as follows:

```
bulk_extractor -o bulk_output terry-work-usb-2009-12-11.E01
```

```
root@kali:~# bulk_extractor -o bulk_output terry-work-usb-2009-12-11.E01
bulk_extractor version: 1.6.0-dev
Hostname: kali
Input file: terry-work-usb-2009-12-11.E01
Output directory: bulk_output
Disk Size: 2097152000
Threads: 4
 8:13:52 Offset 67MB (3.20%) Done in  0:02:35 at 08:16:27
 8:13:53 Offset 150MB (7.20%) Done in  0:01:21 at 08:15:14
 8:13:54 Offset 234MB (11.20%) Done in  0:00:58 at 08:14:52
 8:13:55 Offset 318MB (15.20%) Done in  0:00:46 at 08:14:41
 8:13:56 Offset 402MB (19.20%) Done in  0:00:39 at 08:14:35
 8:13:57 Offset 486MB (23.20%) Done in  0:00:34 at 08:14:31
 8:13:58 Offset 570MB (27.20%) Done in  0:00:29 at 08:14:27
 8:13:59 Offset 654MB (31.20%) Done in  0:00:26 at 08:14:25
 8:13:59 Offset 738MB (35.20%) Done in  0:00:22 at 08:14:21
 8:14:00 Offset 822MB (39.20%) Done in  0:00:20 at 08:14:20
 8:14:01 Offset 905MB (43.20%) Done in  0:00:18 at 08:14:19
 8:14:01 Offset 989MB (47.20%) Done in  0:00:16 at 08:14:17
 8:14:02 Offset 1073MB (51.20%) Done in  0:00:14 at 08:14:16
 8:14:02 Offset 1157MB (55.20%) Done in  0:00:12 at 08:14:14
 8:14:03 Offset 1241MB (59.20%) Done in  0:00:11 at 08:14:14
 8:14:04 Offset 1325MB (63.20%) Done in  0:00:09 at 08:14:13
 8:14:04 Offset 1409MB (67.20%) Done in  0:00:08 at 08:14:12
 8:14:05 Offset 1493MB (71.20%) Done in  0:00:07 at 08:14:12
 8:14:05 Offset 1577MB (75.20%) Done in  0:00:06 at 08:14:11
 8:14:06 Offset 1660MB (79.20%) Done in  0:00:05 at 08:14:11
 8:14:06 Offset 1744MB (83.20%) Done in  0:00:03 at 08:14:09
 8:14:07 Offset 1828MB (87.20%) Done in  0:00:02 at 08:14:09
 8:14:08 Offset 1912MB (91.20%) Done in  0:00:02 at 08:14:10
 8:14:08 Offset 1996MB (95.20%) Done in  0:00:01 at 08:14:09
 8:14:09 Offset 2080MB (99.20%) Done in  0:00:00 at 08:14:09
All data are read; waiting for threads to finish...
Time elapsed waiting for 3 threads to finish:
     (timeout in 60 min.)
```

Once completed, `bulk_extractor` indicates that all threads have finished and provides a summary of the process and even some findings. As seen in the following screen, `bulk_extractor` displays the MD5 hash, the total MB processed and even reports that three email features have been found:

```
All Threads Finished!
Producer time spent waiting: 5.42133 sec.
Average consumer time spent waiting: 4.0313 sec.
MD5 of Disk Image: e07f26954b23db1a44dfd28ecd717da9
Phase 2. Shutting down scanners
Phase 3. Creating Histograms
Elapsed time: 23.3436 sec.
Total MB processed: 2097
Overall performance: 89.8384 MBytes/sec (22.4596 MBytes/sec/thread)
Total email features found: 3
root@kali:~#
```

Viewing results of Bulk_extractor

To view the output of and findings by `bulk_extractor`, we can also display a list of directories within the Terminal by typing `ls -l`. We can see that the `bulk_output` folder has been created by `bulk_extractor`:

```
root@kali:~# ls -l
total 32768
drwxr-xr-x   3 root root     4096 Oct 26 08:14 bulk_output
drwxr-xr--  34 root root     4096 Oct 24 10:58 desktop
drwxr-xr-x   4 root root     4096 Oct 26 08:07 Desktop
drwxr-xr-x   2 root root     4096 Sep 25 13:04 Documents
drwxr-xr-x   3 root root     4096 Oct 26 08:02 Downloads
drwxr-xr--  11 root root     4096 Oct 25 12:01 Foremost_recovery
drwxr-xr-x   2 root root     4096 Oct 26 08:07 Images
drwxr-xr-x   2 root root     4096 Sep 25 13:04 Music
drwxr-xr-x   3 root root     4096 Oct 26 08:24 Pictures
drwxr-xr-x   2 root root     4096 Sep 25 13:04 Public
drwxr-xr--  10 root root     4096 Oct 25 12:03 scalpelOutput
drwxr-xr-x   2 root root     4096 Sep 25 13:04 Templates
-rw-r--r--   1 root root 33499203 Oct 26 08:02 terry-work-usb-2009-12-11.E01
drwxr-xr-x   2 root root     4096 Sep 25 13:04 Videos
root@kali:~#
root@kali:~#
```

We can now list the contents of our output folder (`bulk_output`) by typing `ls -l bulk_output`:

```
root@kali:~# ls -l bulk_output
total 30600
-rw-r--r-- 1 root root        0 Oct 26 08:13 aes_keys.txt
-rw-r--r-- 1 root root        0 Oct 26 08:13 alerts.txt
-rw-r--r-- 1 root root        0 Oct 26 08:14 ccn_histogram.txt
-rw-r--r-- 1 root root        0 Oct 26 08:14 ccn_track2_histogram.txt
-rw-r--r-- 1 root root        0 Oct 26 08:13 ccn_track2.txt
-rw-r--r-- 1 root root        0 Oct 26 08:13 ccn.txt
-rw-r--r-- 1 root root    68140 Oct 26 08:14 domain_histogram.txt
-rw-r--r-- 1 root root  7603392 Oct 26 08:13 domain.txt
-rw-r--r-- 1 root root        0 Oct 26 08:13 elf.txt
-rw-r--r-- 1 root root        0 Oct 26 08:14 email_domain_histogram.txt
-rw-r--r-- 1 root root      260 Oct 26 08:14 email_histogram.txt
-rw-r--r-- 1 root root     1116 Oct 26 08:13 email.txt
-rw-r--r-- 1 root root        0 Oct 26 08:14 ether_histogram.txt
-rw-r--r-- 1 root root        0 Oct 26 08:13 ether.txt
-rw-r--r-- 1 root root      517 Oct 26 08:13 exif.txt
-rw-r--r-- 1 root root        0 Oct 26 08:14 find_histogram.txt
-rw-r--r-- 1 root root        0 Oct 26 08:13 find.txt
-rw-r--r-- 1 root root        0 Oct 26 08:13 gps.txt
-rw-r--r-- 1 root root        0 Oct 26 08:13 httplogs.txt
-rw-r--r-- 1 root root        0 Oct 26 08:14 ip_histogram.txt
-rw-r--r-- 1 root root        0 Oct 26 08:13 ip.txt
-rw-r--r-- 1 root root        0 Oct 26 08:13 jpeg_carved.txt
-rw-r--r-- 1 root root        0 Oct 26 08:13 json.txt
-rw-r--r-- 1 root root        0 Oct 26 08:13 kml.txt
-rw-r--r-- 1 root root        0 Oct 26 08:14 pii_teamviewer.txt
-rw-r--r-- 1 root root        0 Oct 26 08:13 pii.txt
-rw-r--r-- 1 root root        0 Oct 26 08:13 rar.txt
-rw-r--r-- 1 root root    31229 Oct 26 08:14 report.xml
-rw-r--r-- 1 root root        0 Oct 26 08:13 rfc822.txt
-rw-r--r-- 1 root root        0 Oct 26 08:13 sqlite_carved.txt
-rw-r--r-- 1 root root      238 Oct 26 08:14 telephone_histogram.txt
-rw-r--r-- 1 root root      740 Oct 26 08:13 telephone.txt
-rw-r--r-- 1 root root        0 Oct 26 08:13 unrar_carved.txt
-rw-r--r-- 1 root root        0 Oct 26 08:13 unzip_carved.txt
-rw-r--r-- 1 root root        0 Oct 26 08:14 url_facebook-address.txt
```

The list has been split in two to show some of the artifacts found by `bulk_extractor`:

```
-rw-r--r-- 1 root root          0 Oct 26 08:13 ether.txt
-rw-r--r-- 1 root root        517 Oct 26 08:13 exif.txt
-rw-r--r-- 1 root root          0 Oct 26 08:14 find_histogram.txt
-rw-r--r-- 1 root root          0 Oct 26 08:13 find.txt
-rw-r--r-- 1 root root          0 Oct 26 08:13 gps.txt
-rw-r--r-- 1 root root          0 Oct 26 08:13 httplogs.txt
-rw-r--r-- 1 root root          0 Oct 26 08:14 ip_histogram.txt
-rw-r--r-- 1 root root          0 Oct 26 08:13 ip.txt
-rw-r--r-- 1 root root          0 Oct 26 08:13 jpeg_carved.txt
-rw-r--r-- 1 root root          0 Oct 26 08:13 json.txt
-rw-r--r-- 1 root root          0 Oct 26 08:13 kml.txt
-rw-r--r-- 1 root root          0 Oct 26 08:14 pii_teamviewer.txt
-rw-r--r-- 1 root root          0 Oct 26 08:13 pii.txt
-rw-r--r-- 1 root root          0 Oct 26 08:13 rar.txt
-rw-r--r-- 1 root root      31229 Oct 26 08:14 report.xml
-rw-r--r-- 1 root root          0 Oct 26 08:13 rfc822.txt
-rw-r--r-- 1 root root          0 Oct 26 08:13 sqlite_carved.txt
-rw-r--r-- 1 root root        238 Oct 26 08:14 telephone_histogram.txt
-rw-r--r-- 1 root root        740 Oct 26 08:13 telephone.txt
-rw-r--r-- 1 root root          0 Oct 26 08:13 unrar_carved.txt
-rw-r--r-- 1 root root          0 Oct 26 08:13 unzip_carved.txt
-rw-r--r-- 1 root root          0 Oct 26 08:14 url_facebook-address.txt
-rw-r--r-- 1 root root          0 Oct 26 08:14 url_facebook-id.txt
-rw-r--r-- 1 root root    3118516 Oct 26 08:14 url_histogram.txt
-rw-r--r-- 1 root root          0 Oct 26 08:14 url_microsoft-live.txt
-rw-r--r-- 1 root root          0 Oct 26 08:14 url_searches.txt
-rw-r--r-- 1 root root      68107 Oct 26 08:14 url_services.txt
-rw-r--r-- 1 root root   18809144 Oct 26 08:13 url.txt
-rw-r--r-- 1 root root          0 Oct 26 08:13 vcard.txt
-rw-r--r-- 1 root root    1483960 Oct 26 08:13 windirs.txt
-rw-r--r-- 1 root root          0 Oct 26 08:13 winlnk.txt
drwxr-xr-x 3 root root       4096 Oct 26 08:13 winpe_carved
-rw-r--r-- 1 root root       6192 Oct 26 08:13 winpe_carved.txt
-rw-r--r-- 1 root root      76280 Oct 26 08:13 winpe.txt
-rw-r--r-- 1 root root          0 Oct 26 08:13 winprefetch.txt
-rw-r--r-- 1 root root      24457 Oct 26 08:13 zip.txt
root@kali:~#
```

It should be noted that not all listed text files will contain data. Only the ones with numbers larger than 0 to the left of the text filenames will actually contain data.

The text file `ccn.txt` is an abbreviation for **credit card numbers** and will contain credit card information that may have been stolen, illegally used, or stored with possible intention to commit credit card fraud.

If we browse to the output folder location, we can view all extracted data within the individual text files. Viewing the `telephone_histogram.txt` file reveals telephone numbers:

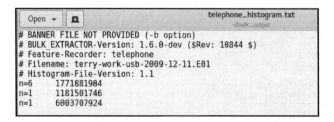

The `url.txt` file reveals many websites and links visited:

```
# BANNER FILE NOT PROVIDED (-b option)
# BULK_EXTRACTOR-Version: 1.6.0-dev ($Rev: 10844 $)
# Feature-Recorder: url
# Filename: terry-work-usb-2009-12-11.E01
# Feature-File-Version: 1.1
4174429 http://www.apple.com/DTDs/PropertyList-1.0.dtd  PLIST 1.0//EN" "http://www.apple.com/DTDs/
PropertyList-1.0.dtd">\x0A<plist versio
4227766 https://domex.nps.edu/domex/svn/src/m57patents/s_time_machine.txt_      s\x00bplist00\xA2
\x01\x02_\x10Ahttps://domex.nps.edu/domex/svn/src/m57patents/s_time_machine.txt_\x10/https://domex.
4227834 https://domex.nps.edu/domex/svn/src/m57patents/ e_machine.txt_\x10/https://domex.nps.edu/
domex/svn/src/m57patents/\x08\x0B0\x00\x00\x00\x00\x00\x00\x01\x01\x00\x00\x00\x00\x00
4289206 https://domex.nps.edu/domex/svn/src/m57patents/s_patent.txt_      s\x00bplist00\xA2\x01\x02_
\x10;https://domex.nps.edu/domex/svn/src/m57patents/s_patent.txt_\x10/https://domex.
4289268 https://domex.nps.edu/domex/svn/src/m57patents/ /s_patent.txt_\x10/https://domex.nps.edu/
domex/svn/src/m57patents/\x08\x0BI\x00\x00\x00\x00\x00\x00\x01\x01\x00\x00\x00\x00\x00
4600502 https://domex.nps.edu/domex/svn/src/m57patents/s_cryptography.txt_      s\x00bplist00\xA2
\x01\x02_\x10Ahttps://domex.nps.edu/domex/svn/src/m57patents/s_cryptography.txt_\x10/https://domex.
4600570 https://domex.nps.edu/domex/svn/src/m57patents/ ptography.txt_\x10/https://domex.nps.edu/
domex/svn/src/m57patents/\x08\x0B0\x00\x00\x00\x00\x00\x00\x01\x01\x00\x00\x00\x00\x00
4620982 https://domex.nps.edu/domex/svn/src/m57patents/s_copyright.txt_ s\x00bplist00\xA2\x01\x02_
\x10>https://domex.nps.edu/domex/svn/src/m57patents/s_copyright.txt_\x10/https://domex.
4621047 https://domex.nps.edu/domex/svn/src/m57patents/ copyright.txt_\x10/https://domex.nps.edu/
domex/svn/src/m57patents/\x08\x0BL\x00\x00\x00\x00\x00\x00\x01\x01\x00\x00\x00\x00\x00
4633315 http://wiki.github.com/bard/mozrepl     gin at:\x0A#        http://wiki.github.com/bard/
mozrepl\x0A#       Once in
4641280 http://www.espn.com     \x00\x00\x00\x00\x00\x00\x00\x00\x00\x00\x00\x00\x00\x00
\x00http://www.espn.com\x0Ahttp://espn.go.
4641300 http://espn.go.com/     ://www.espn.com\x0Ahttp://espn.go.com/\x0Ahttp://sports-a
4641320 http://sports-ak.espn.go.com/nfl/index ://espn.go.com/\x0Ahttp://sports-ak.espn.go.com/
nfl/index\x0Ahttp://espn.go.
4641359 http://espn.go.com/nfl/clubhouse?team=pit         o.com/nfl/index\x0Ahttp://espn.go.com/nfl/
clubhouse?team=pit\x0Ahttp://espn.go.
4641401 http://espn.go.com/nfl/injuries/_/team/pit/pittsburgh-steelers  bhouse?team=pit\x0Ahttp://
espn.go.com/nfl/injuries/_/team/pit/pittsburgh-steelers\x0Ahttp://www.slas
4641464 http://www.slashdot.org sburgh-steelers\x0Ahttp://www.slashdot.org\x0Ahttp://hardware
4641488 http://hardware.slashdot.org/ ww.slashdot.org\x0Ahttp://hardware.slashdot.org/\x0Ahttp://
hardware
```

While this was a simple exercise done with a small evidence file, be sure to have a look at the many others available at `http://digitalcorpora.org/` and see what `bulk_extractor` reveals. Try downloading as many of the images as possible if your bandwidth and storage permit, and also use the other tools we'll use in other chapters.

Summary

In this chapter, we learned about file recovery and data extraction using three readily-available tools within Kali Linux. We first performed file carving using the very impressive Foremost, which searched the entire image for supported file types within the file header and footers. We then did the same using the newer Scalpel, but had to make a slight modification by selecting the file types we wished to carve. Both Foremost and Scalpel presented us with an `audit.txt` file summarizing the carve list and its details along with subfolders containing the actual evidence.

Bulk_extractor is a wonderful tool that carves data and also finds useful information such as email addresses, visited URLs, Facebook URLs, credit card numbers, and a variety of other information. Bulk_extractor is great for investigations requiring file recovery and carving, together with either Foremost or Scalpel, or even both.

Now that we've covered file carving and recovery, let's move on to something more analytical. In the next chapter, we'll take a look at exploring RAM and the paging file as part of memory forensics, using the very powerful volatility. See you there!

7
Memory Forensics with Volatility

In the previous chapters, we looked at the various types of memory. This included RAM and the swap, or paging, file, which is an area of the hard disk drive which, although slower, functions as RAM. We also discussed the issue of RAM being volatile, meaning that the data in the RAM is easily lost when there is no longer electrical charge or current to the RAM. With the data on RAM being the most volatile, it ranks high in the *order of volatility* and must be forensically acquired and preserved as a matter of high priority.

Many types of data and forensic artifacts reside in RAM and the paging file. As discussed earlier, login passwords, user information, running and hidden processes, and even encrypted passwords are just some of the many types of interesting data that can be found when performing RAM analysis, further compounding the need for memory forensics.

In this chapter, we will look at the very powerful Volatility Framework and its many uses in memory forensics.

About the Volatility Framework

The Volatility Framework is an open source, cross-platform, incident response framework that comes with many useful plugins that provide the investigator with a wealth of information from a snapshot of memory, also known as a **memory dump**. The concept of Volatility has been around for a decade, and apart from analyzing running and hidden processes, is also a very popular choice for malware analysis.

To create a memory dump, several tools such as FTK imager, CAINE, Helix, and **LiME** (an acronym for **Linux Memory Extractor**) can be used to acquire the memory image, or memory dump, and then be investigated and analyzed by the tools within the Volatility Framework.

The Volatility Framework can be run on any operating system (32- and 64-bit) that supports Python, including:

- Windows XP, 7, 8,8.1, and Windows 10
- Windows Server 2003, 2008, 2012/R2, and 2016
- Linux 2.6.11 - 4.2.3 (including Kali, Debian, Ubuntu, CentOS, and more)
- macOS Leopard (10.5.x) and Snow Leopard (10.12.x)

Volatility supports several memory dump formats (both 32- and 64-bit), including:

- Windows crash and hibernation dumps (Windows 7 and earlier)
- VirtualBox
- VMWare `.vmem` dump
- VMware saved state and suspended dumps—`.vmss`/`.vmsn`
- Raw physical memory—`.dd`
- Direct physical memory dump over IEEE 1394 FireWire
- **Expert Witness Format (EWF)**—`.E01`
- **QEMU (Quick Emulator)**

Volatility even allows for conversion between these formats and boasts of being able to accomplish everything similar tools can.

Downloading test images for use with Volatility

For this chapter, we'll be using a Windows XP image named `cridex.vmem`, which can be downloaded directly from `https://github.com/volatilityfoundation/volatility/wiki/Memory-Samples`.

Select the link with the **Description** column, **Malware - Cridex** to download the
`cridex.vmem` image:

Memory Samples

iMHLv2 edited this page on Jun 29 · 7 revisions

This is a list of publicly available memory samples for testing purposes.

Description	OS
Art of Memory Forensics Images	Assorted Windows, Linux, and Mac
Mac OSX 10.8.3 x64	Mac Mountain Lion 10.8.3 x64
Jackcr's forensic challenge	Windows XP x86 and Windows 2003 SP0 x86 (4 images)
GrrCon forensic challenge ISO (also see PDF questions)	Windows XP x86
Malware Cookbook DVD	Black Energy, CoreFlood, Laqma, Prolaco, Sality, Silent Banker, Tigger, Zeus, etc
Malware - Cridex	Windows XP SP2 x86
Malware - Shylock	Windows XP SP3 x86
Malware - R2D2 (pw: infected)	Windows XP SP2 x86
Windows 7 x64	Windows 7 SP1 x64
NIST (5 samples)	Windows XP SP2, 2003 SP0, and Vista Beta 2 (all x86)

There are many other images on this page that are also publicly available
for analysis. To practice working with the Volatility Framework and
further enhance your analytical skills, you may wish to download as many
as you like and use the various plugins available in Volatility.

Image location

As we'll soon see, all plugins in the Volatility Framework are used through the Terminal. To make access to the image file easier by not having to specify a lengthy path to the image, we have moved the cridex.vmem image to the Desktop:

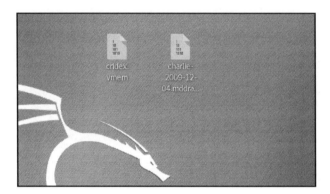

We can also change the directory to the Desktop and then run the Volatility Framework and its plugins from there. To do this, we open a new Terminal and type the following command:

```
cd Desktop
```

We can also view the contents of the Desktop to ensure that the cridex.vmem file is present by typing ls -l:

```
root@kali:~# cd Desktop
root@kali:~/Desktop# ls -l
total 2619384
drwxr-xr-x 6 root root       4096 Nov  9 05:18 CFSI
-rwxrwxr-x 1 root root 2145366016 Dec  4  2009 charlie-2009-12-04.mddramimage
-rw------- 1 root root  536870912 Aug  1  2012 cridex.vmem
drwxr-xr-x 8 root root       4096 Nov  9 05:54 Memory Dumps
root@kali:~/Desktop# 
```

Using Volatility in Kali Linux

To start the Volatility Framework, click on the **All Applications** button at the bottom of the sidebar and type volatility in the search bar:

Clicking on the **volatility** icon starts the program in a Terminal. When Volatility starts, we see that the version being used is 2.6 and also presents us with options for use:

```
 File   Edit   View   Search   Terminal   Help
Volatility Foundation Volatility Framework 2.6
Usage: Volatility - A memory forensics analysis platform.

Options:
  -h, --help              list all available options and their default values.
                          Default values may be set in the configuration file
                          (/etc/volatilityrc)
  --conf-file=/root/.volatilityrc
```

For a complete list of all plugins at your fingertips, open a separate Terminal and run the volatility -h command, rather than having to scroll to the top of the Terminal that you are using to run Volatility plugin commands:

```
root@kali:~# volatility -h
Volatility Foundation Volatility Framework 2.6
Usage: Volatility - A memory forensics analysis platform.

Options:
  -h, --help              list all available options and their default values.
                          Default values may be set in the configuration file
                          (/etc/volatilityrc)
  --conf-file=/root/.volatilityrc
                          User based configuration file
  -d, --debug             Debug volatility
  --plugins=PLUGINS       Additional plugin directories to use (colon separated)
  --info                  Print information about all registered objects
  --cache-directory=/root/.cache/volatility
                          Directory where cache files are stored
  --cache                 Use caching
  --tz=TZ                 Sets the (Olson) timezone for displaying timestamps
                          using pytz (if installed) or tzset
  -f FILENAME, --filename=FILENAME
```

The following screenshot shows a snippet of some of the many plugins within the Volatility Framework:

```
                                         root@kali: ~
File  Edit  View  Search  Terminal  Help

        Supported Plugin Commands:

            amcache          Print AmCache information
            apihooks         Detect API hooks in process and kernel memory
            atoms            Print session and window station atom tables
            atomscan         Pool scanner for atom tables
            auditpol         Prints out the Audit Policies from HKLM\SECURITY\Policy\PolAdtEv
            bigpools         Dump the big page pools using BigPagePoolScanner
            bioskbd          Reads the keyboard buffer from Real Mode memory
            cachedump        Dumps cached domain hashes from memory
            callbacks        Print system-wide notification routines
            clipboard        Extract the contents of the windows clipboard
            cmdline          Display process command-line arguments
            cmdscan          Extract command history by scanning for _COMMAND_HISTORY
            connections      Print list of open connections [Windows XP and 2003 Only]
            connscan         Pool scanner for tcp connections
            consoles         Extract command history by scanning for _CONSOLE_INFORMATION
            crashinfo        Dump crash-dump information
            deskscan         Poolscaner for tagDESKTOP (desktops)
            devicetree       Show device tree
            dlldump          Dump DLLs from a process address space
            dlllist          Print list of loaded dlls for each process
            driverirp        Driver IRP hook detection
            drivermodule     Associate driver objects to kernel modules
            driverscan       Pool scanner for driver objects
```

This list comes in handy when performing analysis as each plugin comes with its own short description. The following screenshot shows a snippet of the `help` command, which gives a description of the `imageinfo` plugin:

```
imageinfo          Identify information for the image
```

The format for using plugins in Volatility is:

```
volatility –f [filename] [plugin] [options]
```

As seen in the previous section, to use the `imageinfo` plugin, we would type:

```
volatility –f cridex.vmem imageinfo
```

Choosing a profile in Volatility

All operating systems store information in RAM, however, they may be situated in different locations within the memory, according to the operating system used. In Volatility, we must choose a profile that best identifies the type of operating system and service pack that helps Volatility in identifying locations that store artifacts and useful information.

Choosing a profile is relatively simple, as volatility does all the work for us, using the `imageinfo` plugin.

The imageinfo plugin

This plugin gives information about the images used, including the suggested operating system and `Image Type (Service Pack)`, the `Number of Processors` used, and the date and time of the image.

The following command is used:

```
volatility -f cridex.vmem imageinfo
```

```
root@kali:~/Desktop# volatility -f cridex.vmem imageinfo
Volatility Foundation Volatility Framework 2.6
INFO    : volatility.debug    : Determining profile based on KDBG search...
          Suggested Profile(s) : WinXPSP2x86, WinXPSP3x86 (Instantiated with WinXPSP2x86)
                     AS Layer1 : IA32PagedMemoryPae (Kernel AS)
                     AS Layer2 : FileAddressSpace (/root/Desktop/cridex.vmem)
                      PAE type : PAE
                           DTB : 0x2fe000L
                          KDBG : 0x80545ae0L
          Number of Processors : 1
     Image Type (Service Pack) : 3
                KPCR for CPU 0 : 0xffdff000L
             KUSER_SHARED_DATA : 0xffdf0000L
           Image date and time : 2012-07-22 02:45:08 UTC+0000
     Image local date and time : 2012-07-21 22:45:08 -0400
```

The `imageinfo` output shows the `Suggested Profile(s)` as `WinXPSP2x86` and `WinXPSP3x86`:

- **WinXP**: Windows XP
- **SP2/SP3**: Service Pack 2/Service Pack 3
- **x86**: 32 bit architecture

```
Volatility Foundation Volatility Framework 2.6
INFO    : volatility.debug    : Determining profile based on KDBG search...
          Suggested Profile(s) : WinXPSP2x86, WinXPSP3x86 (Instantiated with WinXPSP2x86)
                     AS Layer1 : IA32PagedMemoryPae (Kernel AS)
```

The image type, or service pack, is displayed as 3, suggesting that this is a Windows XP, Service Pack 3, 32-bit (x86) operating system that will be used as the profile for the case:

```
root@kali:~/Desktop# volatility imageinfo -f cridex.vmem
Volatility Foundation Volatility Framework 2.6
INFO     : volatility.debug    : Determining profile based on KDBG search...
          Suggested Profile(s) : WinXPSP2x86, WinXPSP3x86 (Instantiated with WinXPSP2x86)
                    AS Layer1 : IA32PagedMemoryPae (Kernel AS)
                    AS Layer2 : FileAddressSpace (/root/Desktop/cridex.vmem)
                    PAE type : PAE
                         DTB : 0x2fe000L
                        KDBG : 0x80545ae0L
         Number of Processors : 1
    Image Type (Service Pack) : 3
          KPCR for CPU 0 : 0xffdff000L
```

Once the profile has been chosen, we can now proceed with using Volatility plugins for analysis of the cridex.vmem image.

Process identification and analysis

To identify and link connected processes, their IDs, times started, and offset locations within the memory image, we will be using the following four plugins to get us started:

- pslist
- pstree
- psscan
- psxview

The pslist command

This tool not only displays a list of all running processes, but also gives useful information such as the **Process ID (PID)** and the **Parent PID (PPID)**, and also shows the time the processes were started. In the screenshot displayed in this section, we can see the System, winlogon.exe, services.exe, svchost.exe, and explorer.exe services are all started first and then followed by reader_sl.exe, alg.exe, and finally wuauclt.exe.

The PID identifies the process and the PPID identifies the parent of the process. Looking at the `pslist` output, we can see that the `winlogon.exe` process has a PID of 608 and a PPID of 368. The PPID's of the `services.exe` and the `lsass.exe` processes (directly after the `winlogon.exe` process) are both 608, indicating that `winlogon.exe` is in fact the PPID for both `services.exe` and `lsass.exe`.

For those new to process IDs and processes themselves, a quick Google search can assist with identification and description information. It is also useful to become familiar with many of the startup processes in order to readily point out processes that may be unusual or suspect.

The timing and order of the processes should also be noted as these may assist in investigations. In the following screenshot, we can see that several processes, including `explorer.exe`, `spoolsv.exe`, and `reader_sl.exe`, all started at the same time of 02:42:36 UTC+0000. We can also tell that `explorer.exe` is the PPID of `reader_sl.exe`.

Adding to this analysis, we can see that there are two instances of `wuauclt.exe` with `svchost.exe` as the PPID.

The `pslist` command used, is as follows:

```
volatility --profile=WinXPSP3x86 -f cridex.vmem pslist
```

```
root@kali:~/Desktop# volatility --profile=WinXPSP3x86 -f cridex.vmem pslist
Volatility Foundation Volatility Framework 2.6
Offset(V)   Name                   PID   PPID   Thds   Hnds   Sess  Wow64  Start
---------   ----------             ----  -----  -----  -----  ----  -----  -----
0x823c89c8  System                   4      0     53    240   ------      0
0x822f1020  smss.exe               368      4      3     19   ------      0  2012-07-22 02:42:31 UTC+0000
0x822a0598  csrss.exe              584    368      9    326      0         0  2012-07-22 02:42:32 UTC+0000
0x82298700  winlogon.exe           608    368     23    519      0         0  2012-07-22 02:42:32 UTC+0000
0x81e2ab28  services.exe           652    608     16    243      0         0  2012-07-22 02:42:32 UTC+0000
0x81e2a3b8  lsass.exe              664    608     24    330      0         0  2012-07-22 02:42:32 UTC+0000
0x82311360  svchost.exe            824    652     20    194      0         0  2012-07-22 02:42:33 UTC+0000
0x81e29ab8  svchost.exe            908    652      9    226      0         0  2012-07-22 02:42:33 UTC+0000
0x823001d0  svchost.exe           1004    652     64   1118      0         0  2012-07-22 02:42:33 UTC+0000
0x821dfda0  svchost.exe           1056    652      5     60      0         0  2012-07-22 02:42:33 UTC+0000
0x82295650  svchost.exe           1220    652     15    197      0         0  2012-07-22 02:42:35 UTC+0000
0x821dea70  explorer.exe          1484   1464     17    415      0         0  2012-07-22 02:42:36 UTC+0000
0x81eb17b8  spoolsv.exe           1512    652     14    113      0         0  2012-07-22 02:42:36 UTC+0000
0x81e7bda0  reader_sl.exe         1640   1484      5     39      0         0  2012-07-22 02:42:36 UTC+0000
0x820e8da0  alg.exe                788    652      7    104      0         0  2012-07-22 02:43:01 UTC+0000
0x821fcda0  wuauclt.exe           1136   1004      8    173      0         0  2012-07-22 02:43:46 UTC+0000
0x8205bda0  wuauclt.exe           1588   1004      5    132      0         0  2012-07-22 02:44:01 UTC+0000
root@kali:~/Desktop#
```

The pstree command

Another process identification command that can be used to list processes is the pstree command. This command shows the same list of processes as the pslist command but indentation is also used to identify child and parent processes.

In the following screenshot, the last two processes listed are explorer.exe and reader_sl.exe. The explorer.exe is not indented, while reader_sl is indented, indicating that sl_reader is the child process and explorer.exe is the parent process:

```
root@kali:~/Desktop# volatility --profile=WinXPSP3x86 -f cridex.vmem pstree
Volatility Foundation Volatility Framework 2.6
Name                                    Pid    PPid   Thds   Hnds Time
-------------------------------------- ------ ------ ------ ------ ----
 0x823c89c8:System                         4      0     53    240 1970-01-01 00:00:00 UTC+0000
. 0x822f1020:smss.exe                    368      4      3     19 2012-07-22 02:42:31 UTC+0000
.. 0x82298700:winlogon.exe               608    368     23    519 2012-07-22 02:42:32 UTC+0000
... 0x81e2ab28:services.exe              652    608     16    243 2012-07-22 02:42:32 UTC+0000
.... 0x821dfda0:svchost.exe             1056    652      5     60 2012-07-22 02:42:33 UTC+0000
.... 0x81eb17b8:spoolsv.exe             1512    652     14    113 2012-07-22 02:42:36 UTC+0000
.... 0x81e29ab8:svchost.exe              908    652      9    226 2012-07-22 02:42:33 UTC+0000
.... 0x823001d0:svchost.exe             1004    652     64   1118 2012-07-22 02:42:33 UTC+0000
..... 0x8205bda0:wuauclt.exe            1588   1004      5    132 2012-07-22 02:44:01 UTC+0000
..... 0x821fcda0:wuauclt.exe            1136   1004      8    173 2012-07-22 02:43:46 UTC+0000
.... 0x82311360:svchost.exe              824    652     20    194 2012-07-22 02:42:33 UTC+0000
.... 0x820e8da0:alg.exe                  788    652      7    104 2012-07-22 02:43:01 UTC+0000
.... 0x82295650:svchost.exe             1220    652     15    197 2012-07-22 02:42:35 UTC+0000
... 0x81e2a3b8:lsass.exe                 664    608     24    330 2012-07-22 02:42:32 UTC+0000
.. 0x822a0598:csrss.exe                  584    368      9    326 2012-07-22 02:42:32 UTC+0000
0x821dea70:explorer.exe                 1484   1464     17    415 2012-07-22 02:42:36 UTC+0000
. 0x81e7bda0:reader_sl.exe              1640   1484      5     39 2012-07-22 02:42:36 UTC+0000
root@kali:~/Desktop#
```

The psscan command

After viewing the list of running processes, we run the psscan command by typing:

```
volatility --profile=WinXPSP3x86 -f cridex.vmem psscan
```

The psscan command displays inactive and even hidden processes that can be used by malware, such as rootkits, and are well known for doing just that to evade discovery by users and antivirus programs.

The output of both the `pslist` and `psscan` commands should be compared to observe any anomalies:

```
root@kali:~/Desktop# volatility --profile=WinXPSP3x86 -f cridex.vmem psscan
Volatility Foundation Volatility Framework 2.6
Offset(P)          Name              PID   PPID PDB        Time created                  Time exited

------------------ ----------------- ----- ---- ---------- ----------------------------- -------------

0x0000000002029ab8 svchost.exe        908   652 0x079400e0 2012-07-22 02:42:33 UTC+0000
0x000000000202a3b8 lsass.exe          664   608 0x079400a0 2012-07-22 02:42:32 UTC+0000
0x000000000202ab28 services.exe       652   608 0x07940080 2012-07-22 02:42:32 UTC+0000
0x000000000207bda0 reader_sl.exe     1640  1484 0x079401e0 2012-07-22 02:42:36 UTC+0000
0x00000000020b17b8 spoolsv.exe       1512   652 0x079401c0 2012-07-22 02:42:36 UTC+0000
0x000000000225bda0 wuauclt.exe       1588  1004 0x07940200 2012-07-22 02:44:01 UTC+0000
0x00000000022e8da0 alg.exe            788   652 0x07940140 2012-07-22 02:43:01 UTC+0000
0x00000000023dea70 explorer.exe      1484  1464 0x079401a0 2012-07-22 02:42:36 UTC+0000
0x00000000023dfda0 svchost.exe       1056   652 0x07940120 2012-07-22 02:42:33 UTC+0000
0x00000000023fcda0 wuauclt.exe       1136  1004 0x07940180 2012-07-22 02:43:46 UTC+0000
0x0000000002495650 svchost.exe       1220   652 0x07940160 2012-07-22 02:42:35 UTC+0000
0x0000000002498700 winlogon.exe       608   368 0x07940060 2012-07-22 02:42:32 UTC+0000
0x00000000024a0598 csrss.exe          584   368 0x07940040 2012-07-22 02:42:32 UTC+0000
0x00000000024f1020 smss.exe           368     4 0x07940020 2012-07-22 02:42:31 UTC+0000
0x00000000025001d0 svchost.exe       1004   652 0x07940100 2012-07-22 02:42:33 UTC+0000
0x0000000002511360 svchost.exe        824   652 0x079400c0 2012-07-22 02:42:33 UTC+0000
```

The psxview plugin

As with `psscan`, the `psxview` plugin is used to find and list hidden processes. With `psxview` however, a variety of scans are run, including `pslist` and `psscan`.

The command to run the `psxview` plugin is as follows:

```
volatility --profile=WinXPSP3x86 -f cridex.vmem psxview
```

```
root@kali:~/Desktop# volatility --profile=WinXPSP3x86 -f cridex.vmem psxview
Volatility Foundation Volatility Framework 2.6
Offset(P)  Name                   PID pslist psscan thrdproc pspcid csrss session deskthrd ExitTime
---------- -------------------- ----- ------ ------ -------- ------ ----- ------- --------
0x02498700 winlogon.exe           608 True   True   True     True   True  True    True
0x02511360 svchost.exe            824 True   True   True     True   True  True    True
0x022e8da0 alg.exe                788 True   True   True     True   True  True    True
0x020b17b8 spoolsv.exe           1512 True   True   True     True   True  True    True
0x0202ab28 services.exe           652 True   True   True     True   True  True    True
0x02495650 svchost.exe           1220 True   True   True     True   True  True    True
0x0207bda0 reader_sl.exe         1640 True   True   True     True   True  True    True
0x025001d0 svchost.exe           1004 True   True   True     True   True  True    True
0x02029ab8 svchost.exe            908 True   True   True     True   True  True    True
0x023fcda0 wuauclt.exe           1136 True   True   True     True   True  True    True
0x0225bda0 wuauclt.exe           1588 True   True   True     True   True  True    True
0x0202a3b8 lsass.exe              664 True   True   True     True   True  True    True
0x023dea70 explorer.exe          1484 True   True   True     True   True  True    True
0x023dfda0 svchost.exe           1056 True   True   True     True   True  True    True
0x024f1020 smss.exe               368 True   True   True     True   False False   False
0x025c89c8 System                   4 True   True   True     True   False False   False
0x024a0598 csrss.exe              584 True   True   True     True   False True    True
root@kali:~/Desktop#
```

Analyzing network services and connections

Volatility can be used to identify and analyze active, terminated, and hidden connections along with ports and processes. All protocols are supported and Volatility also reveals details of ports used by processes including the times they were started.

For these purposes, we use the following three commands:

- `connections`
- `connscan`
- `sockets`

The connections command

The `connections` command lists active connections at that point in time, displaying local and remote IP addresses with ports and PID. The `connections` command is used only for Windows XP and 2003 Server (both 32- and 64-bit). The `connections` command is used as follows:

```
volatility --profile=WinXPSP3x86 -f cridex.vmem connections
```

```
root@kali:~/Desktop# volatility --profile=WinXPSP3x86 -f cridex.vmem connections
Volatility Foundation Volatility Framework 2.6
Offset(V)  Local Address          Remote Address          Pid
---------- ---------------------- ----------------------- ---
0x81e87620 172.16.112.128:1038       41.168.5.140:8080        1484
root@kali:~/Desktop#
```

The connscan command

The `connections` command displayed only one connection as active at that time. To display a list of connections that have been terminated, the `connscan` command is used. The `connscan` command is also only for Windows XP and 2003 Server (both 32 and 64-bit) systems:

```
volatility --profile=WinXPSP3x86 -f cridex.vmem connscan
```

```
root@kali:~/Desktop# volatility --profile=WinXPSP3x86 -f cridex.vmem connscan
Volatility Foundation Volatility Framework 2.6
Offset(P)  Local Address          Remote Address          Pid
---------- ---------------------- ----------------------- ---
0x02087620 172.16.112.128:1038       41.168.5.140:8080        1484
0x023a8008 172.16.112.128:1037      125.19.103.198:8080       1484
root@kali:~/Desktop#
```

Using the `connscan` command, we are able to see that the same local address was previously connected to another `Remote Address` with the IP `125.19.103.198:8080`. The `Pid` of `1484` tells us that connection was made by the `explorer.exe` process (as displayed using the `pslist` command earlier).

More information on remote addresses can be obtained using IP lookup tools and websites such as `http://whatismyipaddress.com/ip-lookup`:

By clicking on the **Get IP Details** button, the following results are presented to us including **ISP** name, **Continent** and **Country** details, along with a map showing approximate location of the device with that IP:

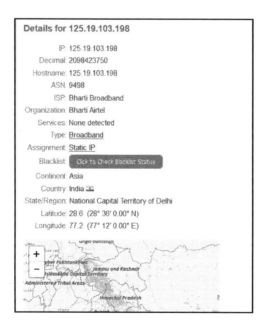

The sockets plugin

The `sockets` plugin can be used to give additional connectivity information listening sockets. Although UDP and TCP are the only protocols listed in the output in the following screenshot, the `sockets` command supports all protocols:

```
root@kali:~/Desktop#
root@kali:~/Desktop# volatility --profile=WinXPSP3x86 -f cridex.vmem sockets
Volatility Foundation Volatility Framework 2.6
Offset(V)       PID   Port  Proto Protocol     Address         Create Time
---------- -------- ------ ------ -------- -------------- --------------
0x81ddb780      664    500     17 UDP          0.0.0.0         2012-07-22 02:42:53 UTC+0000
0x82240d08     1484   1038      6 TCP          0.0.0.0         2012-07-22 02:44:45 UTC+0000
0x81dd7618     1220   1900     17 UDP          172.16.112.128  2012-07-22 02:43:01 UTC+0000
0x82125610      788   1028      6 TCP          127.0.0.1       2012-07-22 02:43:01 UTC+0000
0x8219cc08        4    445      6 TCP          0.0.0.0         2012-07-22 02:42:31 UTC+0000
0x81ec23b0      908    135      6 TCP          0.0.0.0         2012-07-22 02:42:33 UTC+0000
0x82276878        4    139      6 TCP          172.16.112.128  2012-07-22 02:42:38 UTC+0000
0x82277460        4    137     17 UDP          172.16.112.128  2012-07-22 02:42:38 UTC+0000
0x81e76620     1004    123     17 UDP          127.0.0.1       2012-07-22 02:43:01 UTC+0000
0x82172808      664      0    255 Reserved     0.0.0.0         2012-07-22 02:42:53 UTC+0000
0x81e3f460        4    138     17 UDP          172.16.112.128  2012-07-22 02:42:38 UTC+0000
0x821f0630     1004    123     17 UDP          172.16.112.128  2012-07-22 02:43:01 UTC+0000
0x822cd2b0     1220   1900     17 UDP          127.0.0.1       2012-07-22 02:43:01 UTC+0000
0x82172c50      664   4500     17 UDP          0.0.0.0         2012-07-22 02:42:53 UTC+0000
0x821f0d00        4    445     17 UDP          0.0.0.0         2012-07-22 02:42:31 UTC+0000
root@kali:~/Desktop#
```

DLL analysis

DLLs (Dynamic Link Libraries) are specific to Microsoft and contain code that can be used by multiple programs simultaneously. Inspection of a process's running DDLs and the version information of files and products may assist in correlating processes. Processes and DLL information should also be analyzed as they relate to user accounts.

For these tasks we can use the following plugins:

- `verinfo`
- `dlllist`
- `getsids`

The verinfo command

This command lists version information (`verinfo`) about **PE** (**portable executable**) files. The output of this file is usually quite lengthy and so can be run in a separate Terminal, should the investigator not wish to continuously scroll through the current Terminal to review past plugin command lists and output.

The `verinfo` command is used as follows:

```
volatility --profile=WinXPSP3x86 -f cridex.vmem verinfo
```

```
root@kali:~/Desktop# volatility --profile=WinXPSP3x86 -f cridex.vmem verinfo
Volatility Foundation Volatility Framework 2.6
\SystemRoot\System32\smss.exe
C:\WINDOWS\system32\ntdll.dll
\??\C:\WINDOWS\system32\csrss.exe
C:\WINDOWS\system32\ntdll.dll
C:\WINDOWS\system32\CSRSRV.dll
C:\WINDOWS\system32\basesrv.dll
C:\WINDOWS\system32\winsrv.dll
C:\WINDOWS\system32\GDI32.dll
C:\WINDOWS\system32\KERNEL32.dll
C:\WINDOWS\system32\USER32.dll
    File version    : 5.1.2600.5512
    Product version : 5.1.2600.5512
    Flags           :
    OS              : Windows NT
    File Type       : Dynamic Link Library
    File Date       :
    CompanyName : Microsoft Corporation
    FileDescription : Windows XP USER API Client DLL
    FileVersion : 5.1.2600.5512 (xpsp.080413-2105)
    InternalName : user32
    LegalCopyright : \xa9 Microsoft Corporation. All rights reserved.
    OriginalFilename : user32
    ProductName : Microsoft\xae Windows\xae Operating System
    ProductVersion : 5.1.2600.5512
C:\WINDOWS\system32\sxs.dll
    File version    : 5.1.2600.5512
    Product version : 5.1.2600.5512
    Flags           :
    OS              : Windows NT
    File Type       : Dynamic Link Library
    File Date       :
    CompanyName : Microsoft Corporation
    FileDescription : Fusion 2.5
    FileVersion : 5.1.2600.5512 (xpsp.080413-2111)
```

The dlllist plugin

The `dlllist` plugin lists all running DLLs at that time in memory. DLLs are composed of code that can be used by multiple programs simultaneously.

The `dlllist` command is used as follows:

```
volatility --profile=WinXPSP3x86 -f cridex.vmem dlllist
```

```
root@kali:~/Desktop# volatility --profile=WinXPSP3x86 -f cridex.vmem dlllist
Volatility Foundation Volatility Framework 2.6
************************************************************************
System pid:      4
Unable to read PEB for task.
************************************************************************
smss.exe pid:    368
Command line : \SystemRoot\System32\smss.exe


Base           Size     LoadCount Path
---------- ---------- ---------- ----
0x48580000     0xf000     0xffff \SystemRoot\System32\smss.exe
0x7c900000     0xaf000    0xffff C:\WINDOWS\system32\ntdll.dll
************************************************************************
csrss.exe pid:   584
Command line : C:\WINDOWS\system32\csrss.exe ObjectDirectory=\Windows SharedSection=1024,
3072,512 Windows=On SubSystemType=Windows ServerDll=basesrv,1 ServerDll=winsrv:UserServer
DllInitialization,3 ServerDll=winsrv:ConServerDllInitialization,2 ProfileControl=Off MaxR
equestThreads=16
Service Pack 3

Base           Size     LoadCount Path
---------- ---------- ---------- ----
0x4a680000     0x5000     0xffff \??\C:\WINDOWS\system32\csrss.exe
0x7c900000     0xaf000    0xffff C:\WINDOWS\system32\ntdll.dll
0x75b40000     0xb000     0xffff C:\WINDOWS\system32\CSRSRV.dll
0x75b50000     0x10000       0x3 C:\WINDOWS\system32\basesrv.dll
0x75b60000     0x4b000       0x2 C:\WINDOWS\system32\winsrv.dll
0x77f10000     0x49000       0x5 C:\WINDOWS\system32\GDI32.dll
0x7c800000     0xf6000      0x10 C:\WINDOWS\system32\KERNEL32.dll
0x7e410000     0x91000       0x6 C:\WINDOWS\system32\USER32.dll
0x7e720000     0xb0000       0x1 C:\WINDOWS\system32\sxs.dll
0x77dd0000     0x9b000       0x5 C:\WINDOWS\system32\ADVAPI32.dll
0x77e70000     0x92000       0x3 C:\WINDOWS\system32\RPCRT4.dll
```

The getsids command

All users can also be uniquely identified by a **Security Identifier** (**SID**). The `getsids` command has four very useful items in the order in which the processes were started (refer to `pslist` and `pstree` command screenshots).

The format for the `getsids` command output is:

```
[Process] (PID) [SID] (User)
```

The first result in the list for example, lists:

```
System (4) : S - 1 - 5- 18 (User)
```

- `System`: process
- `(4)`: PID
- `S - 1 - 5- 18`: SID
- `User`: Local system

 If the last number in the SID is in the range of 500, this indicates a user with administrator privileges. For example, `S - 1 - 5- 32-544` (administrators).

The `getsids` command is used as follows:

```
volatility --profile=WinXPSP3x86 -f cridex.vmem getsids
```

```
root@kali:~/Desktop# volatility --profile=WinXPSP3x86 -f cridex.vmem getsids
Volatility Foundation Volatility Framework 2.6
System (4): S-1-5-18 (Local System)
System (4): S-1-5-32-544 (Administrators)
System (4): S-1-1-0 (Everyone)
System (4): S-1-5-11 (Authenticated Users)
smss.exe (368): S-1-5-18 (Local System)
smss.exe (368): S-1-5-32-544 (Administrators)
smss.exe (368): S-1-1-0 (Everyone)
smss.exe (368): S-1-5-11 (Authenticated Users)
csrss.exe (584): S-1-5-18 (Local System)
csrss.exe (584): S-1-5-32-544 (Administrators)
csrss.exe (584): S-1-1-0 (Everyone)
csrss.exe (584): S-1-5-11 (Authenticated Users)
winlogon.exe (608): S-1-5-18 (Local System)
winlogon.exe (608): S-1-5-32-544 (Administrators)
winlogon.exe (608): S-1-1-0 (Everyone)
winlogon.exe (608): S-1-5-11 (Authenticated Users)
services.exe (652): S-1-5-18 (Local System)
services.exe (652): S-1-5-32-544 (Administrators)
services.exe (652): S-1-1-0 (Everyone)
services.exe (652): S-1-5-11 (Authenticated Users)
lsass.exe (664): S-1-5-18 (Local System)
lsass.exe (664): S-1-5-32-544 (Administrators)
lsass.exe (664): S-1-1-0 (Everyone)
lsass.exe (664): S-1-5-11 (Authenticated Users)
svchost.exe (824): S-1-5-18 (Local System)
svchost.exe (824): S-1-5-32-544 (Administrators)
svchost.exe (824): S-1-1-0 (Everyone)
svchost.exe (824): S-1-5-11 (Authenticated Users)
svchost.exe (908): S-1-5-20 (NT Authority)
svchost.exe (908): S-1-5-20 (NT Authority)
svchost.exe (908): S-1-1-0 (Everyone)
svchost.exe (908): S-1-5-32-545 (Users)
svchost.exe (908): S-1-5-6 (Service)
```

Scrolling down the `getsids` output, we can see that a user named `Robert` with an SID of `S-1-5-21-79336058` (non-administrator) has started or accessed `explorer.exe`, PID `1484`:

```
svchost.exe (1220): S-1-5-5-0-52148 (Logon Session)
svchost.exe (1220): S-1-2-0 (Local (Users with the ability to log in locally))
svchost.exe (1220): S-1-1-0 (Everyone)
svchost.exe (1220): S-1-5-11 (Authenticated Users)
svchost.exe (1220): S-1-2-0 (Local (Users with the ability to log in locally))
svchost.exe (1220): S-1-5-32-545 (Users)
explorer.exe (1484): S-1-5-21-789336058-261478967-1417001333-1003 (Robert)
explorer.exe (1484): S-1-5-21-789336058-261478967-1417001333-513 (Domain Users)
explorer.exe (1484): S-1-1-0 (Everyone)
explorer.exe (1484): S-1-5-32-544 (Administrators)
explorer.exe (1484): S-1-5-32-545 (Users)
explorer.exe (1484): S-1-5-4 (Interactive)
explorer.exe (1484): S-1-5-11 (Authenticated Users)
```

Registry analysis

Information about every user, setting, program, and the Windows operating system itself can be found within the registry. Even hashed passwords can be found in the registry. In the Windows registry analysis, we will be using the following two plugins.

- `hivescan`
- `hivelist`

The hivescan plugin

The `hivescan` plugin displays the physical locations of available registry hives.

The command to run `hivescan` is as follows:

<pre>**volatility --profile=WinXPSP3x86 -f cridex.vmem hivescan**

```
root@kali:~/Desktop#
root@kali:~/Desktop# volatility --profile=WinXPSP3x86 -f cridex.vmem hivescan
Volatility Foundation Volatility Framework 2.6
Offset(P)
----------
0x02a7d008
0x02ac3b60
0x02e4b008
0x07669510
0x076699b8
0x0777f008
0x0777f9e8
0x08519b60
0x08a838d0
0x08e2db60
0x08e624d0
0x093f8b60
0x0a5a9b60
```

The hivelist plugin

For more detailed (and helpful) information on registry hives and locations within RAM, the `hivelist` plugin can be used. The `hivelist` command shows the details of `Virtual` and `Physical` addresses along with the easier readable plaintext names and locations.

The command used to run `hivelist` is as follows:

```
volatility --profile=WinXPSP3x86 -f cridex.vmem hivelist
```

```
root@kali:~/Desktop# volatility --profile=WinXPSP3x86 -f cridex.vmem hivelist
Volatility Foundation Volatility Framework 2.6
Virtual     Physical    Name
----------  ----------  ----
0xe18e5b60 0x093f8b60 \Device\HarddiskVolume1\Documents and Settings\Robert\Local Setting
s\Application Data\Microsoft\Windows\UsrClass.dat
0xe1a19b60 0x0a5a9b60 \Device\HarddiskVolume1\Documents and Settings\Robert\NTUSER.DAT
0xe18398d0 0x08a838d0 \Device\HarddiskVolume1\Documents and Settings\LocalService\Local S
ettings\Application Data\Microsoft\Windows\UsrClass.dat
0xe18614d0 0x08e624d0 \Device\HarddiskVolume1\Documents and Settings\LocalService\NTUSER.
DAT
0xe183bb60 0x08e2db60 \Device\HarddiskVolume1\Documents and Settings\NetworkService\Local
 Settings\Application Data\Microsoft\Windows\UsrClass.dat
0xe17f2b60 0x08519b60 \Device\HarddiskVolume1\Documents and Settings\NetworkService\NTUSE
R.DAT
0xe1570510 0x07669510 \Device\HarddiskVolume1\WINDOWS\system32\config\software
0xe1571008 0x0777f008 \Device\HarddiskVolume1\WINDOWS\system32\config\default
0xe15709b8 0x076699b8 \Device\HarddiskVolume1\WINDOWS\system32\config\SECURITY
0xe15719e8 0x0777f9e8 \Device\HarddiskVolume1\WINDOWS\system32\config\SAM
0xe13ba008 0x02e4b008 [no name]
0xe1035b60 0x02ac3b60 \Device\HarddiskVolume1\WINDOWS\system32\config\system
0xe102e008 0x02a7d008 [no name]
root@kali:~/Desktop#
```

Password dumping

The location of the **Security Accounts Manager (SAM)** file is also listed using the `hivelist` plugin, shown in the following screenshot. The SAM file contains hashed passwords for usernames in Windows machines. The path to the SAM file is seen in the following screenshot as `Windows\system32\config\SAM`. This file cannot be accessed by users within Windows while the system is on. This can be further used to acquire the hashed passwords in the SAM file to crack passwords using a `wordlist` along with password-cracking tools such as **John the Ripper**, also available in Kali Linux:

```
0xe15719e8 0x0777f9e8 \Device\HarddiskVolume1\WINDOWS\system32\config\SAM
```

Timeline of events

Volatility can produce a list of timestamped events, which is essential to any investigation. To produce this list, we will use the `timeliner` plugin.

The timeliner plugin

The `timeliner` plugin helps investigators by providing a timeline of all the events that took place when the image was acquired. Although we have an idea of what took place within this scenario, many other dumps may be quite large and far more detailed and complex.

The `timeliner` plugin groups details by time and includes process, PID, process offset, DDLs used, registry details, and other useful information.

To run the `timeliner` command, we type the following:

```
volatility --profile=WinXPSP3x86 -f cridex.vmem timeliner
```

```
root@kali:~/Desktop# volatility --profile=WinXPSP3x86 -f cridex.vmem timeliner
Volatility Foundation Volatility Framework 2.6
2012-07-22 02:45:08 UTC+0000|[LIVE RESPONSE]| (System time)|
2012-07-22 02:42:32 UTC+0000|[PROCESS]| winlogon.exe| PID: 608/PPID: 368/POffset: 0x02498700
2012-07-22 02:42:32 UTC+0000|[PROCESS LastTrimTime]| winlogon.exe| PID: 608/PPID: 368/POffset: 0x02498700
2012-07-22 02:42:32 UTC+0000|[Handle (Key)]| MACHINE| winlogon.exe PID: 608/PPID: 368/POffset: 0x02498700
2012-02-18 20:11:36 UTC+0000|[Handle (Key)]| MACHINE\SOFTWARE\CLASSES| winlogon.exe PID: 608/PPID: 368/POffset: 0x
02498700
2011-04-13 00:40:42 UTC+0000|[Handle (Key)]| USER\.DEFAULT| winlogon.exe PID: 608/PPID: 368/POffset: 0x02498700
2011-04-13 00:38:27 UTC+0000|[Handle (Key)]| MACHINE\SYSTEM\CONTROLSET001\SERVICES\WINSOCK2\PARAMETERS\PROTOCOL_CA
TALOG9| winlogon.exe PID: 608/PPID: 368/POffset: 0x02498700
2011-04-13 00:38:21 UTC+0000|[Handle (Key)]| MACHINE\SYSTEM\CONTROLSET001\SERVICES\WINSOCK2\PARAMETERS\NAMESPACE_C
ATALOG5| winlogon.exe PID: 608/PPID: 368/POffset: 0x02498700
2011-04-12 20:31:50 UTC+0000|[Handle (Key)]| MACHINE\SOFTWARE\MICROSOFT\WINDOWS NT\CURRENTVERSION\WINLOGON\NOTIFY\
CRYPT32CHAIN| winlogon.exe PID: 608/PPID: 368/POffset: 0x02498700
2011-04-12 20:31:50 UTC+0000|[Handle (Key)]| MACHINE\SOFTWARE\MICROSOFT\WINDOWS NT\CURRENTVERSION\WINLOGON\NOTIFY\
CRYPTNET| winlogon.exe PID: 608/PPID: 368/POffset: 0x02498700
2011-04-13 00:41:01 UTC+0000|[Handle (Key)]| MACHINE\SOFTWARE\MICROSOFT\WINDOWS NT\CURRENTVERSION\DRIVERS32| winlo
gon.exe PID: 608/PPID: 368/POffset: 0x02498700
2011-04-13 00:41:53 UTC+0000|[Handle (Key)]| MACHINE\SOFTWARE\MICROSOFT\WINDOWS NT\CURRENTVERSION\WINLOGON\NOTIFY\
SCLGNTFY| winlogon.exe PID: 608/PPID: 368/POffset: 0x02498700
2012-07-22 02:29:50 UTC+0000|[Handle (Key)]| MACHINE\SYSTEM\CONTROLSET001\CONTROL\LSA| winlogon.exe PID: 608/PPID:
 368/POffset: 0x02498700
2012-07-22 02:42:33 UTC+0000|[Handle (Key)]| MACHINE\SOFTWARE\MICROSOFT\WINDOWS NT\CURRENTVERSION\WINLOGON| winlog
on.exe PID: 608/PPID: 368/POffset: 0x02498700
2012-07-22 02:42:33 UTC+0000|[Handle (Key)]| MACHINE\SOFTWARE\MICROSOFT\WINDOWS NT\CURRENTVERSION\WINLOGON| winlog
on.exe PID: 608/PPID: 368/POffset: 0x02498700
2012-07-22 02:42:33 UTC+0000|[Handle (Key)]| MACHINE\SOFTWARE\MICROSOFT\WINDOWS NT\CURRENTVERSION\WINLOGON\CREDENT
IALS| winlogon.exe PID: 608/PPID: 368/POffset: 0x02498700
2011-04-13 00:49:16 UTC+0000|[Handle (Key)]| MACHINE\SYSTEM\SETUP| winlogon.exe PID: 608/PPID: 368/POffset: 0x0249
8700
2012-07-22 02:42:35 UTC+0000|[Handle (Key)]| USER| winlogon.exe PID: 608/PPID: 368/POffset: 0x02498700
```

The following is a snippet of the `timeliner` command, when scrolling further through its output:

```
2008-04-13 21:04:09 UTC+0000|[PE HEADER (exe)]| winlogon.exe| Process: winlogon.exe/PID: 608/PPID: 368/Process POf
fset: 0x02498700/DLL Base: 0x01000000
-|[PE DEBUG]| winlogon.exe| Process: winlogon.exe/PID: 608/PPID: 368/Process POffset: 0x02498700/DLL Base: 0x01000
000
2008-04-14 00:11:24 UTC+0000|[PE HEADER (dll)]| ntdll.dll| Process: winlogon.exe/PID: 608/PPID: 368/Process POffse
t: 0x02498700/DLL Base: 0x7c900000
-|[PE DEBUG]| ntdll.dll| Process: winlogon.exe/PID: 608/PPID: 368/Process POffset: 0x02498700/DLL Base: 0x7c900000
2008-04-13 17:26:05 UTC+0000|[PE HEADER (dll)]| odbcint.dll| Process: winlogon.exe/PID: 608/PPID: 368/Process POff
set: 0x02498700/DLL Base: 0x00930000
-|[PE DEBUG]| odbcint.dll| Process: winlogon.exe/PID: 608/PPID: 368/Process POffset: 0x02498700/DLL Base: 0x009300
00
2008-04-14 00:09:35 UTC+0000|[PE HEADER (dll)]| Apphelp.dll| Process: winlogon.exe/PID: 608/PPID: 368/Process POff
set: 0x02498700/DLL Base: 0x77b40000
-|[PE DEBUG]| Apphelp.dll| Process: winlogon.exe/PID: 608/PPID: 368/Process POffset: 0x02498700/DLL Base: 0x77b400
00
2008-04-14 00:10:39 UTC+0000|[PE HEADER (dll)]| PROFMAP.dll| Process: winlogon.exe/PID: 608/PPID: 368/Process POff
set: 0x02498700/DLL Base: 0x75930000
-|[PE DEBUG]| PROFMAP.dll| Process: winlogon.exe/PID: 608/PPID: 368/Process POffset: 0x02498700/DLL Base: 0x759300
00
2008-04-14 00:11:02 UTC+0000|[PE HEADER (dll)]| SHLWAPI.dll| Process: winlogon.exe/PID: 608/PPID: 368/Process POff
set: 0x02498700/DLL Base: 0x77f60000
```

Malware analysis

Adding to Volatility's impressive line-up of plugins is the `malfind` plugin.

The `malfind` plugin, as the name suggests, is used to find, or at least direct the investigator toward hints of, malware that may have been injected into various processes. The output of the `malfind` plugin may be particularly and so should be run in a separate Terminal to avoid constant scrolling when reviewing the output from the other plugin commands.

The command used to run `malfind` is as follows:

```
volatility --profile=WinXPSP3x86 -f cridex.vmem malfind
```

```
root@kali:~/Desktop# volatility --profile=WinXPSP3x86 -f cridex.vmem malfind
Volatility Foundation Volatility Framework 2.6
Process: csrss.exe Pid: 584 Address: 0x7f6f0000
Vad Tag: Vad  Protection: PAGE_EXECUTE_READWRITE
Flags: Protection: 6

0x7f6f0000   c8 00 00 00 91 01 00 00 ff ee ff ee 08 70 00 00   .............p..
0x7f6f0010   08 00 00 00 00 fe 00 00 00 00 10 00 00 20 00 00   ................
0x7f6f0020   00 02 00 00 00 20 00 00 8d 01 00 00 ff ef fd 7f   ................
0x7f6f0030   03 00 08 06 00 00 00 00 00 00 00 00 00 00 00 00   ................

0x7f6f0000 c8000000                ENTER 0x0, 0x0
0x7f6f0004 91                      XCHG ECX, EAX
0x7f6f0005 0100                    ADD [EAX], EAX
0x7f6f0007 00ff                    ADD BH, BH
0x7f6f0009 ee                      OUT DX, AL
0x7f6f000a ff                      DB 0xff
0x7f6f000b ee                      OUT DX, AL
0x7f6f000c 087000                  OR [EAX+0x0], DH
0x7f6f000f 0008                    ADD [EAX], CL
0x7f6f0011 0000                    ADD [EAX], AL
0x7f6f0013 0000                    ADD [EAX], AL
0x7f6f0015 fe00                    INC BYTE [EAX]
0x7f6f0017 0000                    ADD [EAX], AL
0x7f6f0019 0010                    ADD [EAX], DL
0x7f6f001b 0000                    ADD [EAX], AL
0x7f6f001d 2000                    AND [EAX], AL
0x7f6f001f 0000                    ADD [EAX], AL
0x7f6f0021 0200                    ADD AL, [EAX]
0x7f6f0023 0000                    ADD [EAX], AL
0x7f6f0025 2000                    AND [EAX], AL
0x7f6f0027 008d010000ff            ADD [EBP-0xffffff], CL
0x7f6f002d ef                      OUT DX, EAX
0x7f6f002e fd                      STD
0x7f6f002f 7f03                    JG 0x7f6f0034
0x7f6f0031 0008                    ADD [EAX], CL
```

The `malfind` plugin can also be run directly on processes using the -p switch.

As we've discovered, `winlogon.exe` is assigned the PID 608. To run `malfind` on PID 608, we type:

```
volatility --profile=WinXPSP3x86 -f cridex.vmem malfind -p 608
```

```
Process: winlogon.exe Pid: 608 Address: 0x13410000
Vad Tag: VadS Protection: PAGE_EXECUTE_READWRITE
Flags: CommitCharge: 4, MemCommit: 1, PrivateMemory: 1, Protection: 6

0x13410000  00 00 00 00 00 00 00 00 00 00 00 00 00 00 00 00   ................
0x13410010  00 00 00 00 00 00 00 00 00 00 00 00 00 00 00 00   ................
0x13410020  00 00 00 00 00 00 00 00 00 00 00 00 00 00 00 00   ................
0x13410030  00 00 00 00 25 00 25 00 01 00 00 00 00 00 00 00   ....%.%.........

0x13410000 0000            ADD [EAX], AL
0x13410002 0000            ADD [EAX], AL
0x13410004 0000            ADD [EAX], AL
0x13410006 0000            ADD [EAX], AL
0x13410008 0000            ADD [EAX], AL
0x1341000a 0000            ADD [EAX], AL
0x1341000c 0000            ADD [EAX], AL
0x1341000e 0000            ADD [EAX], AL
0x13410010 0000            ADD [EAX], AL
0x13410012 0000            ADD [EAX], AL
0x13410014 0000            ADD [EAX], AL
0x13410016 0000            ADD [EAX], AL
0x13410018 0000            ADD [EAX], AL
0x1341001a 0000            ADD [EAX], AL
0x1341001c 0000            ADD [EAX], AL
0x1341001e 0000            ADD [EAX], AL
0x13410020 0000            ADD [EAX], AL
0x13410022 0000            ADD [EAX], AL
0x13410024 0000            ADD [EAX], AL
0x13410026 0000            ADD [EAX], AL
0x13410028 0000            ADD [EAX], AL
0x1341002a 0000            ADD [EAX], AL
0x1341002c 0000            ADD [EAX], AL
```

Summary

In this chapter, we looked at memory forensics and analysis using some of the many plugins available within the Volatility Framework. One of the first, and most important, steps in working with Volatility is choosing the profile that Volatility will use throughout the analysis. This profile tells Volatility what type of operating system is being used. Once the profile was chosen, we were able to successfully perform process, network, registry, DLL, and even malware analysis using this versatile tool. As we've seen, Volatility can perform several important functions in digital forensics and should be used together with other tools we've used previously to perform in-depth and detailed forensic analysis and investigations.

Be sure to download more publicly available memory images and samples to test your skills in this area. Experiment with as many plugins as you can and of course, be sure to document your findings and consider sharing them online.

In our next chapter, we will move on to another powerful tool that does everything from acquisition to reporting. Let's get started with Autopsy—The Sleuth Kit®.

8
Autopsy – The Sleuth Kit

Autopsy and The Sleuth Kit go hand in hand. Both created by Brian Carrier. The Sleuth Kit is a powerful suite of CLI forensic tools, whereas Autopsy is the GUI that sits on top of The Sleuth Kit, and is accessed through a web browser. The Sleuth Kit supports disk image file types including RAW (DD), EnCase (.01), and **Advanced Forensic Format** (**AFF**).

The Sleuth Kit uses command-line interface tools to perform the following tasks:

- Find and list allocated and unallocated (deleted) files, and even files hidden by rootkits
- Reveal NTFS **Alternate Data Streams** (**ADS**) where files can be concealed within other files
- List files by types
- Display metadata information
- Timeline creation

Autopsy can be run from a Live CD/USB in forensic mode as part of a live analysis in live mode, or it can be used on a dedicated machine to investigate analysis in dead mode.

The topics that we will cover in this chapter include the following:

- A Sample image file used in Autopsy
- Digital forensics with Autopsy
- Creating a new case in Autopsy
- Analysis using Autopsy
- Reopening cases in Autopsy

Introduction to Autopsy – The Sleuth Kit

Autopsy offers GUI access to a variety of investigative command-line tools from The Sleuth Kit, including file analysis, image and file hashing, deleted file recovery, and case management, among other capabilities. Autopsy can be problematic when installing but, fortunately for us, comes built into Kali Linux, and is also very easy to set up and use.

Although the Autopsy browser is based on The Sleuth Kit, features of Autopsy differ when using the Windows version as compared to the Linux version. Some of the official features offered by The Sleuth Kit and Autopsy 2.4 in Kali Linux include:

- **Image analysis**: Analyzing directories and files including sorting files, recovering deleted files, and previewing files
- **File activity timelines**: Creating timelines based on timestamps of files when they were written, accessed, and created
- **Image integrity**: Creating MD5 hashes of the image file used, as well as individual files
- **Hash databases**: Matching digital hashes or fingerprints of unknown files (such as suspected malicious .exe files) against those in the NIST **National Software Reference Library (NSRL)**
- **Events sequencer**: Displaying events sorted by date and time
- **File analysis**: Analyzing the entire image file to display directory and file information and contents
- **Keyword search**: Allows searching using keyword lists and predefined expression lists
- **Metadata analysis**: Allows viewing of metadata details and structures of files that are essential for data recovery

Sample image file used in Autopsy

The image file used for analysis is publicly available for download at `http://dftt.sourceforge.net/`.

The file we will be working with is **JPEG Search Test #1 (Jun '04)**, as shown in the following screenshot:

Test Images:

1. Extended Partition Test (July '03)
2. FAT Keyword Search Test (Aug '03)
3. NTFS Keyword Search Test #1 (Oct '03)
4. EXT3FS Keyword Search Test #1 (Nov '03)
5. FAT Daylight Savings Test (Jan '04)
6. FAT Undelete Test #1 (Feb '04)
7. NTFS Undelete (and leap year) Test #1 (Feb '04)
8. JPEG Search Test #1 (Jun '04)
9. FAT Volume Label Test #1 (Aug '04)
10. NTFS Autodetect Test #1 (Jan '05)
11. Basic Data Carving Test #1 (Mar '05) (by Nick Mikus)
12. Basic Data Carving Test #2 (Mar '05) (by Nick Mikus)
13. Windows Memory Analysis #1 (Jan '06) (by Jesse Kornblum)
14. ISO9660 Interpretation Test #1 (Aug '10)

This image contains several files with changed extensions and other files within them, as seen in the following download description:

Num	Name	MD5	Note
1	alloc\file1.jpg	75b8d0056815a36c3809b46fc84ba6d	A JPEG file with a JPEG extension
2	alloc\file2.dat	de5d83153339931371719f4e5c924eba	A JPEG file with a non-JPEG extension
3	invalid\file3.jpg	1ba4e91591f0541eda255ee26f7533bc	A random file with a JPEG extension
4	invalid\file4.jpg	c8de721182617158e8492121bdad3711	A random file with 0xffd8 as the first two bytes (the JPEG header signature). There is no JPEG footer or other header data.
5	invalid\file5.rtf	86f14fc525648c39d878829f288c0543	A random file with the 0xffd8 signature value in several locations inside of the file.
6	del1\file6.jpg - MFT Entry #32	afd55222024a4e22f7f5a3a665320763	A deleted JPEG file with a JPEG extension.
7	del2\file7.hmm - MFT Entry #31	0c452c5800fcfa7c66027ae89c4f068a	A deleted JPEG file with a non-JPEG extension.
8	archive\file8.zip	d41b56e0a9f84eb2825e73c24cedd963	A ZIP file with a ZIP extension and a JPEG picture named file8.jpg inside of it.
	file8.jpg	f9956284a89156ef6967b49eced9d1b1	A JPEG file that is inside of a ZIP file with a ZIP extension.
9	archive\file9.boo	73c3029066aee9416a5aeb90a5c55321	A ZIP file with a non-ZIP extension and a JPEG picture named file9.jpg inside of it.
	file9.jpg	c5a6917669c77d20f30ecb39d389eb7d	A JPEG file that is inside of a ZIP file with a non-ZIP extension.
10	archive\file10.tar.gz	d4f8cf643141f0c2911c539750e18ef2	A gzipped tar file that contains a JPEG picture named file10.jpg.
	file10.jpg	c476a66ccdc2796b4f6f8e27273dd788	A JPEG file that is inside of a gzipped tar file.
11	misc\file11.dat	f407ab92da959c7ab03292cfe596a99d	A file with 1572 bytes of random data and then a JPEG picture. This was created using the '+' option in the Windows copy.exe tool.
12	misc\file12.doc	61c0b55639e52d1ce82aba834ada2bab	A Word document with the JPEG picture inside of it.
13	misc\file13.dll:here	9b787e63e3b64562730c5aecaab1e1f8	A JPEG file in an ADS.

Be sure to note the location of the downloaded sample file, as this will be required later on.

When investigating hard drives and devices, be sure to always follow proper acquisition procedures and use a write-blocker to avoid tampering with original evidence.

Digital forensics with Autopsy

Now that we have our sample image file downloaded (or perhaps even a forensically acquired image of our own), let's proceed with the analysis using the Autopsy browser by first getting acquainted with the different ways to start Autopsy.

Starting Autopsy

Autopsy can be started in two ways. The first uses the **Applications** menu by clicking on **Applications | 11 - Forensics | autopsy**:

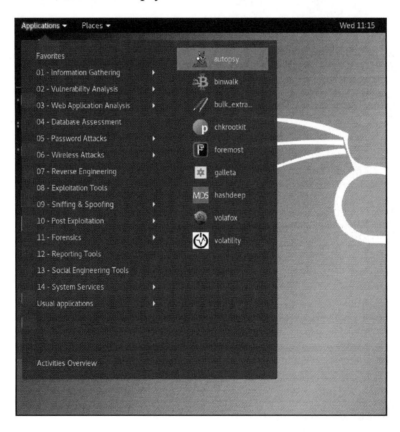

Alternatively, we can click on the Show applications icon (last item in the side menu) and type `autopsy` into the search bar at the top-middle of the screen and then click on the **autopsy** icon:

Once the **autopsy** icon is clicked, a new terminal is opened showing the program information along with connection details for opening the **The Autopsy Forensic Browser**.

In the following screenshot, we can see that the version number is listed as **2.24** with the path to the `Evidence Locker` folder as `/var/lib/autopsy`:

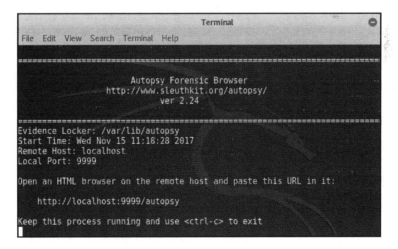

To open the Autopsy browser, position the mouse over the link in the terminal, then right-click and choose **Open Link**, as seen in the following screenshot:

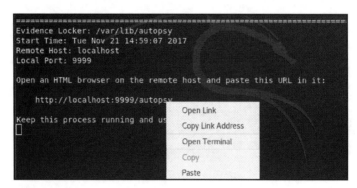

Creating a new case

To create a new case, follow the given steps:

1. When the **Autopsy Forensic Browser** opens, investigators are presented with three options.
2. Click on **NEW CASE**:

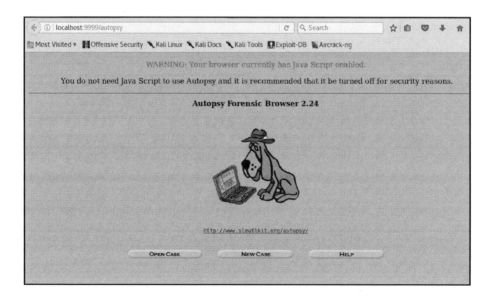

3. Enter details for the **Case Name**, **Description**, and **Investigator Names**. For the **Case Name**, I've entered SP-8-dftt, as it closely matches the image name (8-jpeg-search.dd), which we will be using for this investigation. Once all information is entered, click **NEW CASE**:

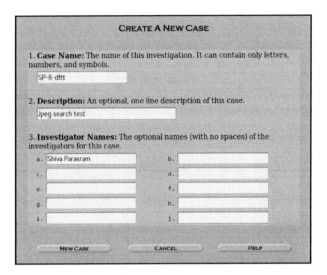

Several investigator name fields are available, as there may be instances where several investigators may be working together.

The locations of the **Case directory** and **Configuration file** are displayed and shown as **created**. It's important to take note of the case directory location, as seen in the screenshot: **Case directory (/var/lib/autopsy/SP-8-dftt/) created**. Click **ADD HOST** to continue:

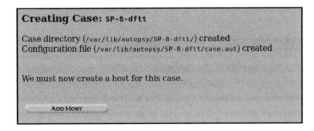

4. Enter the details for the **Host Name** (name of the computer being investigated) and the **Description** of the host.

5. Optional settings:
   - **Time zone**: Defaults to local settings, if not specified
   - **Timeskew Adjustment**: Adds a value in seconds to compensate for time differences
   - **Path of Alert Hash Database**: Specifies the path of a created database of known bad hashes
   - **Path of Ignore Hash Database**: Specifies the path of a created database of known good hashes similar to the NIST NSRL:

1. **Host Name:** The name of the computer being investigated. It can contain only letters, numbers, and symbols.

> host1

2. **Description:** An optional one-line description or note about this computer.

> 10 MB NTFS

3. **Time zone:** An optional timezone value (i.e. EST5EDT). If not given, it defaults to the local setting. A list of time zones can be found in the help files.

4. **Timeskew Adjustment:** An optional value to describe how many seconds this computer's clock was out of sync. For example, if the computer was 10 seconds fast, then enter -10 to compensate.

> 0

5. **Path of Alert Hash Database:** An optional hash database of known bad files.

6. **Path of Ignore Hash Database:** An optional hash database of known good files.

ADD HOST   CANCEL   HELP

6. Click on the **ADD HOST** button to continue.

7. Once the host is added and directories are created, we add the forensic image we want to analyze by clicking the **ADD IMAGE** button:

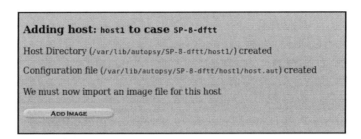

Adding host: host1 **to case** SP-8-dftt

Host Directory (/var/lib/autopsy/SP-8-dftt/host1/) created

Configuration file (/var/lib/autopsy/SP-8-dftt/host1/host.aut) created

We must now import an image file for this host

ADD IMAGE

8. Click on the **ADD IMAGE FILE** button to add the image file:

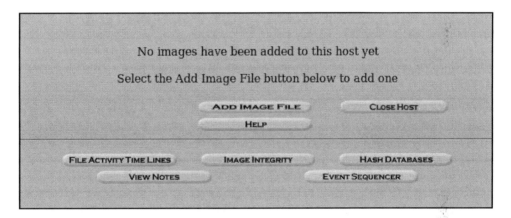

No images have been added to this host yet

Select the Add Image File button below to add one

ADD IMAGE FILE   CLOSE HOST

HELP

FILE ACTIVITY TIME LINES   IMAGE INTEGRITY   HASH DATABASES

VIEW NOTES   EVENT SEQUENCER

9. To import the image for analysis, the full path must be specified. On my machine, I've saved the image file (8-jpeg-search.dd) to the Desktop folder. As such, the location of the file would be /root/Desktop/ 8-jpeg-search.dd.

For the **Import Method,** we choose **Symlink**. This way the image file can be imported from its current location (Desktop) to the Evidence Locker without the risks associated with moving or copying the image file.

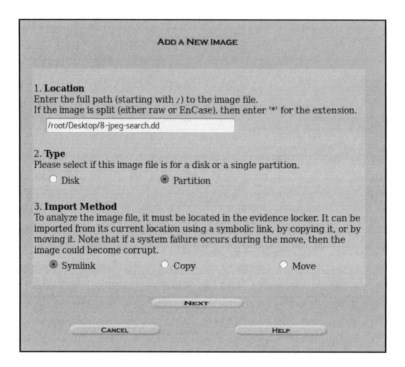

10. If you are presented with the following error message, ensure that the specified image location is correct and that the forward slash (/) is used:

> Invalid wild image (img_path) argument

11. Upon clicking **Next,** the **Image File Details** are displayed. To verify the integrity of the file, select the radio button for **Calculate the hash value for this image,** and select the checkbox next to **Verify hash after importing?**.

12. The **File System Details** section also shows that the image is of an **ntfs** partition.

13. Click on the **ADD** button to continue:

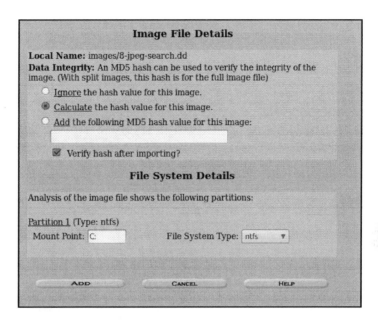

14. After clicking the **ADD** button in the previous screenshot, Autopsy calculates the MD5 hash and links the image into the evidence locker. Press **OK** to continue:

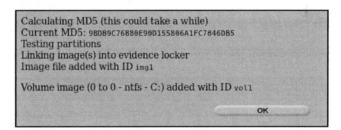

15. At this point, we're just about ready to analyze the image file. If there are multiple cases listed in the gallery area from any previous investigations you may have worked on, be sure to choose the `8-jpeg-search.dd` file and case:

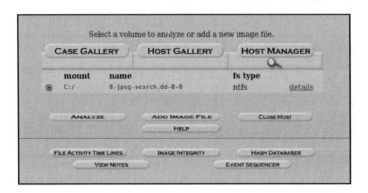

16. Before proceeding, we can click on the **IMAGE DETAILS** option. This screen gives detail such as the image name, volume ID, file format, file system, and also allows for the extraction of ASCII, Unicode, and unallocated data to enhance and provide faster keyword searches. Click on the back button in the browser to return to the previous menu and continue with the analysis:

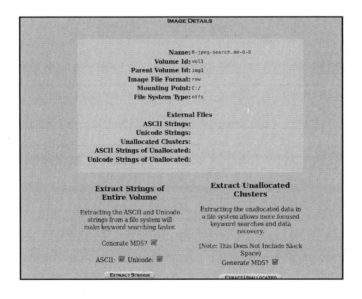

17. Before clicking on the **ANALYZE** button to start our investigation and analysis, we can also verify the integrity of the image by creating an MD5 hash, by clicking on the **IMAGE INTEGRITY** button:

 Several other options exist such as **FILE ACTIVITY TIMELINES, HASH DATABASES,** and so on. We can return to these at any point in the investigation.

18. After clicking on the **IMAGE INTEGRITY** button, the image name and hash are displayed. Click on the **VALIDATE** button to validate the MD5 hash:

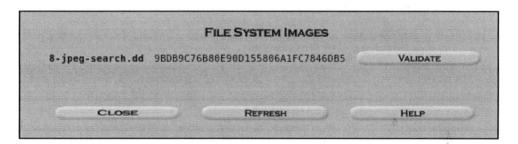

19. The validation results are displayed in the lower-left corner of the Autopsy browser window:

Original MD5: 9BDB9C76B80E90D155806A1FC7846DB5
Current MD5: 9BDB9C76B80E90D155806A1FC7846DB5

Pass

20. We can see that our validation was successful, with matching MD5 hashes displayed in the results. Click on the **CLOSE** button to continue.

21. To begin our analysis, we click on the **ANALYZE** button:

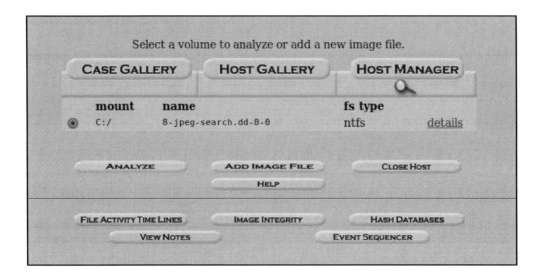

Analysis using Autopsy

Now that we've created our case, added host information with appropriate directories, and added our acquired image, we get to the analysis stage.

After clicking on the **ANALYZE** button (see the previous screenshot), we're presented with several options in the form of tabs, with which to begin our investigation:

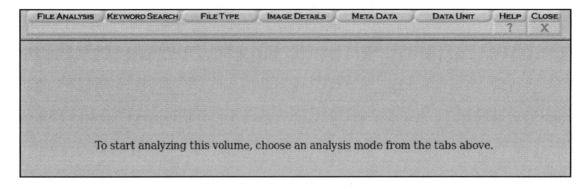

Let's look at the details of the image by clicking on the **IMAGE DETAILS** tab. In the following snippet, we can see the **Volume Serial Number** and the operating system (**Version**) listed as **Windows XP**:

FILE SYSTEM INFORMATION

File System Type: NTFS
Volume Serial Number: 325C284B5C280C63
OEM Name: NTFS
Volume Name: JPEG-SRCH
Version: Windows XP

Next, we click on the **FILE ANALYSIS** tab. This mode opens into **File Browsing Mode,** which allows the examination of directories and files within the image. Directories within the image are listed by default in the main view area:

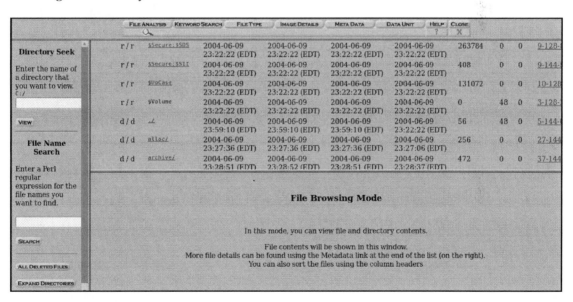

In **File Browsing Mode**, directories are listed with the **Current Directory** specified as C:/.

For each directory and file, there are fields showing when the item was **WRITTEN, ACCESSED, CHANGED,** and **CREATED,** along with its size and **META** data:

- **WRITTEN**: The date and time the file was last written to
- **ACCESSED**: The date and time the file was last accessed (only the date is accurate)
- **CHANGED**: The date and time the descriptive data of the file was changed
- **CREATED**: The data and time the file was created
- **META**: Metadata describing the file and information about the file:

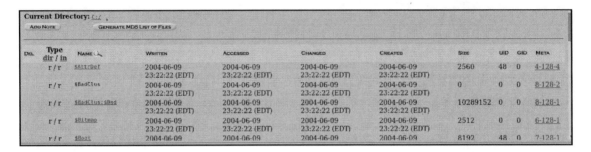

For integrity purposes, MD5 hashes of all files can be made by clicking on the **GENERATE MD5 LIST OF FILES** button.

Investigators can also make notes about files, times, anomalies, and so on, by clicking on the **ADD NOTE** button:

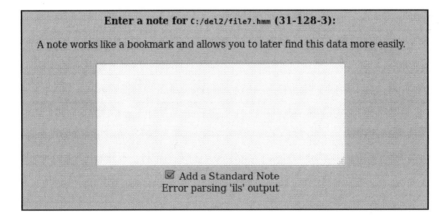

The left pane contains four main features that we will be using:

- **Directory Seek**: Allows for the searching of directories
- **File Name Search**: Allows for the searching of files by Perl expressions or filenames
- **ALL DELETED FILES**: Searches the image for deleted files
- **EXPAND DIRECTORIES**: Expands all directories for easier viewing of contents

By clicking on **EXPAND DIRECTORIES**, all contents are easily viewable and accessible within the left pane and main window. The **+** next to a directory indicates that it can be further expanded to view subdirectories (**++**) and their contents:

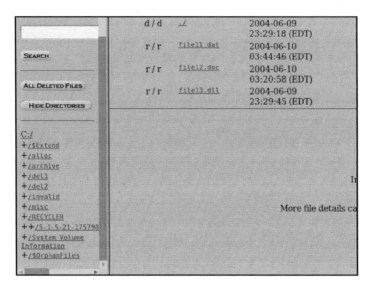

To view deleted files, we click on the **ALL DELETED FILES** button in the left pane. Deleted files are marked in red and also adhere to the same format of **WRITTEN**, **ACCESSED**, **CHANGED**, and **CREATED** times.

From the following screenshot, we can see that the image contains two deleted files:

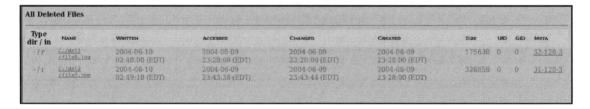

We can also view more information about this file by clicking on its **META** entry. By viewing the metadata entries of a file (last column to the right), we can also view the hexadecimal entries for the file, which may give the true file extensions, even if the extension was changed.

In the preceding screenshot, the second deleted file (file7.hmm) has a peculiar file extension of .hmm.

Click on the **META** entry (**31-128-3**) to view the metadata:

```
$FILE_NAME Attribute Values:
Flags: Archive
Name: file7.hmm
Parent MFT Entry: 47 Sequence: 1
Allocated Size: 327168 Actual Size: 326859
Created: 2004-06-09 23:28:00.742657600 (EDT)
File Modified: 2004-06-10 02:49:18.000000000 (EDT)
MFT Modified: 2004-06-09 23:28:00.842801600 (EDT)
Accessed: 2004-06-09 23:28:00.842801600 (EDT)

Attributes:
$STANDARD_INFORMATION (16-0) Name: N/A Resident size: 72
$FILE_NAME (48-4) Name: N/A Resident size: 84
$DATA (128-3) Name: N/A Non-Resident size: 326859 init_size: 326859
1066 1067 1068 1069 1070 1071 1072 1073
1074 1075 1076 1077 1078 1079 1080 1081
1082 1083 1084 1085 1086 1087 1088 1089
1090 1091 1092 1093 1094 1095 1096 1097
1098 1099 1100 1101 1102 1103 1104 1105
1106 1107 1108 1109 1110 1111 1112 1113
1114 1115 1116 1117 1118 1119 1120 1121
1122 1123 1124 1125 1126 1127 1128 1129
1130 1131 1132 1133 1134 1135 1136 1137
```

Under the **Attributes** section, click on the first cluster labelled **1066** to view header information of the file:

```
                                                                     3
Cluster: 1066
Status: Not Allocated

ASCII Contents of Cluster 1066 in 8-jpeg-search.dd-0-0


.....JFIF....... ........C................................
.....................}.........!1A..Qa."q.2....#B...R..$3br.
.....%&'()*456789:CDEFGHIJSTUVWXYZcdefghijstuvwxyz...................
.....................w........!1..AQ.aq."2...B....      #3R..br.
.$4.%.....&'()*56789:CDEFGHI
```

We can see that the first entry is **.JFIF**, which is an abbreviation for **JPEG File Interchange Format**. This means that the `file7.hmm` file is an image file, but had its extension changed to `.hmm`.

Sorting files

Inspecting the metadata of each file may not be practical with large evidence files. For such an instance, the **FILE TYPE** feature can be used. This feature allows for the examination of existing (allocated), deleted (unallocated), and hidden files. Click on the **FILE TYPE** tab to continue:

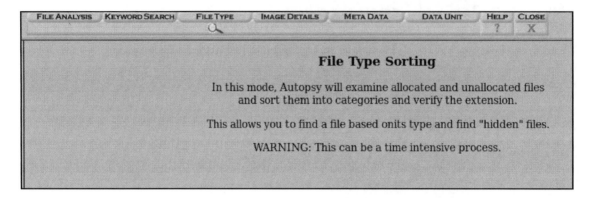

Click **Sort files into categories by type** (leave the default-checked options as they are) and then click **OK** to begin the sorting process:

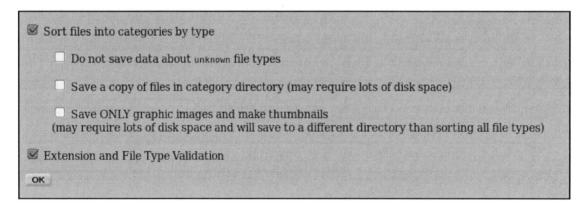

Once sorting is complete, a results summary is displayed. In the following snippet, we can see that there are five **Extension Mismatches**:

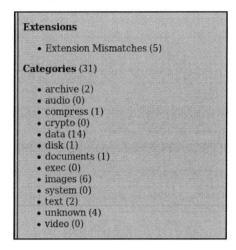

To view the sorted files, we must manually browse to the location of the `output` folder, as Autopsy 2.4 does not support viewing of sorted files. To reveal this location, click on **View Sorted Files** in the left pane:

 The `output` folder locations will vary depending on the information specified by the user when first creating the case, but can usually be found at `/var/lib/autopsy/<case name>/<host name>/output/sorter-vol#/index.html`.

Once the `index.html` file has been opened, click on the **Extension Mismatch** link:

Extension Mismatch

C:/alloc/file2.dat
  JPEG image data, JFIF standard 1.01, aspect ratio, density 1x1, segment length 16, baseline, precision 8, 437x365, frames 3 (Ext: dat)
  Image: /var/lib/autopsy/SP-8-dftt/11/images/8-jpeg-search.dd Inode: 28-128-3

C:/archive/file9.boo
  gzip ERROR: Exec `gzip' failed, No such file or directory (Zip archive data, at least v2.0 to extract) (Ext: boo)
  Image: /var/lib/autopsy/SP-8-dftt/11/images/8-jpeg-search.dd Inode: 40-128-3

C:/del2/file7.hmm
  JPEG image data, JFIF standard 1.01, aspect ratio, density 1x1, segment length 16, baseline, precision 8, 698x752, frames 3 (Ext: hmm)
  Image: /var/lib/autopsy/SP-8-dftt/11/images/8-jpeg-search.dd Inode: 31-128-3

C:/invalid/file3.jpg
  ASCII text (Ext: jpg)
  Image: /var/lib/autopsy/SP-8-dftt/11/images/8-jpeg-search.dd Inode: 35-128-3

C:/misc/file13.dll:here
  JPEG image data, JFIF standard 1.01, aspect ratio, density 1x1, segment length 16, baseline, precision 8, 518x563, frames 3 (Ext: dll:here)
  Image: /var/lib/autopsy/SP-8-dftt/11/images/8-jpeg-search.dd Inode: 44-128-5

The five listed files with mismatched extensions should be further examined by viewing metadata content, with notes added by the investigator.

Reopening cases in Autopsy

Cases are usually ongoing and can easily be restarted by starting Autopsy and clicking on **OPEN CASE**:

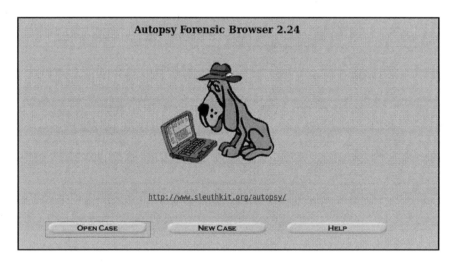

In the **CASE GALLERY**, be sure to choose the correct case name and, from there, continue your examination:

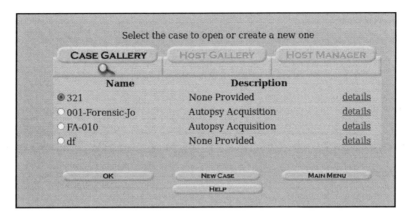

Summary

In this chapter, we looked at forensics using the **Autopsy Forensic Browser** with The Sleuth Kit. Compared to individual tools, Autopsy has case management features and supports various types of file analysis, searching, and sorting of allocated, unallocated, and hidden files. Autopsy can also perform hashing on a file and directory levels to maintain evidence integrity.

Next up, we have analysis of internet and network artifacts using another very powerful GUI tool called **Xplico**. See you in Chapter 9, *Network and Internet Capture Analysis with Xplico*.

9

Network and Internet Capture Analysis with Xplico

Xplico is an open source, GUI **Network Forensics Analysis Tool (NFAT)** that focuses on extracting artifacts from network and internet captures.

Captures of network and internet traffic are obtained directly in Xplico using its live acquisition feature but can also be done using tools within Kali Linux such as Wireshark and Ettercap. These network acquisition files are saved as `.pcap` or **packet capture** files that are then uploaded to Xplico and decoded automatically using its IP decoder and decoder manager components.

Some of the protocols that we can investigate using Xplico include, but are not limited to:

- **Transmission Control Protocol (TCP)**
- **User Datagram Protocol (UDP)**
- **Hypertext Transfer Protocol (HTTP)**
- **File Transfer Protocol (FTP)**
- **Trivial FTP (TFTP)**
- **Session Initiation Protocol (SIP)**
- **Post Office Protocol (POP)**
- **Internet Map Access Protocol (IMAP)**
- **Simple Mail Transfer Protocol (SMTP)**

Data contained in network and internet packet captures, and even live acquisition, can contain artifacts such as:

- HTTP traffic such as websites browsed
- Email
- Facebook chats
- RTP and VoIP
- Printed files

 Traffic encrypted using **Secure Sockets Layer** (**SSL**) cannot be currently viewed with Xplico.

Software required

Xplico comes with many versions of Linux. Xplico usually requires some updates to run, depending on the versions of Kali used. For this chapter I recommend using Kali Linux 2016.1 or 2016.2. I also recommend using Kali in a virtual environment when using Xplico as incorrectly updating Kali could *break* it. Users may also wish to use the snapshot feature before updating Kali Linux which saves the current working state of the machine that can be easily rolled back to, in the event that the distribution breaks.

 Kali Linux 2016.1 can be downloaded from `https://cdimage.kali.org/kali-2016.1/`.

Kali Linux 2016.2 can be downloaded from `https://cdimage.kali.org/kali-2016.2/`.

Should you run into difficulties updating Kali or running Xplico (which happens sometimes) consider downloading and running DEFT Linux 8.2 in a virtual environment. Beginners may find that Xplico may be easier to work with in DEFT Linux as there are GUI menu items to start the Apache and Xplico services options, whereas these have to be typed into the Terminal in Kali Linux.

 DEFT Linux 8.2 can be downloaded from `http://na.mirror.garr.it/mirrors/deft/`.

Starting Xplico in Kali Linux

Updating Kali is simple as the commands remain the same when updating throughout different versions (2016.x and 2017.x).

In a new Terminal, we type `apt-get update` and press *Enter*. The `sudo apt-get update` command may have to be used to provide admin privileges if the former does not run successfully.

We then attempt to install Xplico by typing `apt-get install xplico` (or `sudo apt-get install xplico`):

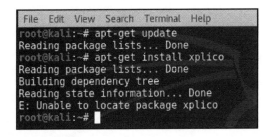

If an error is encountered, as seen in the following screenshot, we must update the Kali Linux repositories by first updating our sources list and then running the `apt-get update` command again. To update the sources list, type the `leafpad /etc/apt/sources.list` command which opens up the file for us to edit:

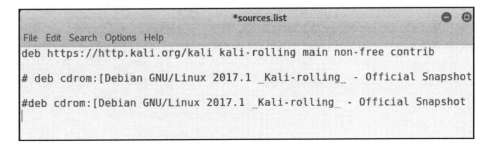

At the top of the file, enter the following repository location:

```
deb https://http.kali.org/kali kali-rolling main non-free contrib
```

Once the repository location is entered, click **File**, then **Save**, and then close the list.

Be sure to remove any # symbols in front of the text as this ignores any text that follows.

After closing the list file, return to the Terminal and run the `apt-get update` command once more:

```
root@kali:~# leafpad /etc/apt/sources.list
root@kali:~#
root@kali:~# apt-get update
Get:1 https://archive-2.kali.org/kali kali-rolling InRelease [30.5 kB]
Get:2 https://archive-2.kali.org/kali kali-rolling/main amd64 Packages [15.6 MB]
Get:3 https://archive-2.kali.org/kali kali-rolling/non-free amd64 Packages [166 kB]
Get:4 https://archive-2.kali.org/kali kali-rolling/contrib amd64 Packages [113 kB]
Fetched 16.0 MB in 11s (1,360 kB/s)
Reading package lists... Done
root@kali:~#
```

After Kali has been updated, run the `apt-get install xplico` command. Be sure to press *Y* to continue when prompted:

```
root@kali:~#
root@kali:~# apt-get install xplico
Reading package lists... Done
Building dependency tree
Reading state information... Done
The following additional packages will be installed:
  lame libapache2-mod-php7.0 libmp3lame0 libndpi4 librecode0 libsox-fmt-alsa libsox-fmt-base libsox2
  php-sqlite3 php7.0-cli php7.0-common php7.0-json php7.0-mysql php7.0-opcache php7.0-readline
  php7.0-sqlite3 python3-psycopg2 recode sox
Suggested packages:
  lame-doc php-pear libsox-fmt-all python-psycopg2-doc
The following NEW packages will be installed:
  lame libndpi4 librecode0 libsox-fmt-alsa libsox-fmt-base libsox2 php-sqlite3 php7.0-sqlite3
  python3-psycopg2 recode sox xplico
The following packages will be upgraded:
  libapache2-mod-php7.0 libmp3lame0 php7.0-cli php7.0-common php7.0-json php7.0-mysql php7.0-opcache
  php7.0-readline
8 upgraded, 12 newly installed, 0 to remove and 1613 not upgraded.
Need to get 7,743 kB of archives.
After this operation, 16.2 MB of additional disk space will be used.
Do you want to continue? [Y/n]
```

Once Xplico has been installed, we must start the Apache 2 and Xplico services. In the Terminal, enter the following two commands:

- `service apache2 start`
- `service xplico start`

Once these steps have been completed, the Xplico can now be accessed by clicking **Applications** | **11 - Forensics** | **xplico**:

A browser window opens immediately after with the URL, `localhost:9876/users/login`.

Starting Xplico in DEFT Linux 8.2

As mentioned earlier, DEFT Linux 8.2 should be run as a virtual host. This process is not as in-depth as installing Kali Linux (as covered in Chapter 2, *Installing Kali Linux*) because DEFT can be used as a live forensic acquisition distribution.

Once the DEFT Linux ISO image had been downloaded (from http://na.mirror.garr.it/mirrors/deft/), open VirtualBox, click **New**, and enter the following details:

- **Name**: Deft 8.2
- **Type**: **Linux**
- **Version**: **Ubuntu (64-bit)**

Now, after filling in the appropriate information, follow these steps:

1. Assign 4 or more GBs of RAM.
2. Leave the default option of **Create a virtual hard disk now** and click **Create**.
3. Leave the default option of **VDI (VirtualBox Disk Image)** and click **Next**.
4. Leave the default option of **Dynamically allocated**, click **Next**, and click on **Create**.
5. Click the green start arrow on the **VirtualBox Manager** screen to start the VM.

When prompted to **Select start-up disk,** click the browse-folder icon and browse to the downloaded DEFT Linux 8.2 ISO image, then click **Start**:

This brings the user to the DEFT splash screen. Select **English** for your language and select **DEFT Linux 8 live**:

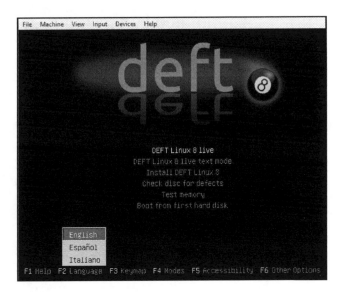

After DEFT Linux boots and loads the desktop, click the DEFT menu button on the lower left corner, then click the **Service** menu, and then click **Apache start**. Repeat this process to get to the **Service** menu and then click **Xplico start**:

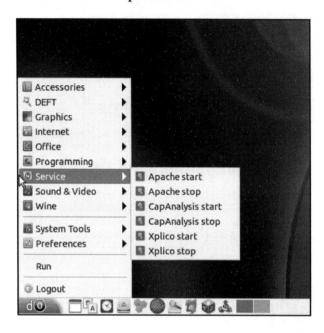

Finally, start Xplico by clicking the DEFT button, then go to the **DEFT** menu, across to **Network Forensics**, and click **Xplico**:

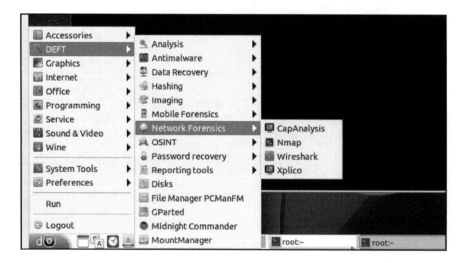

This brings us to the very same Xplico web interface GUI also available in Kali Linux:

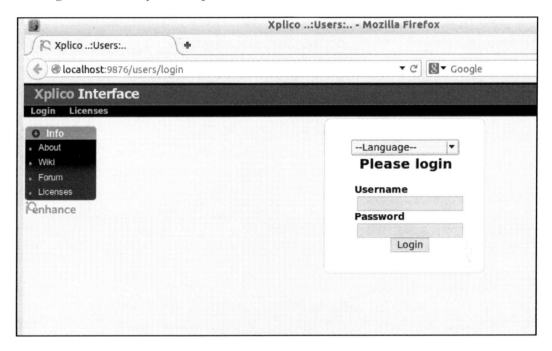

Packet capture analysis using Xplico

Whether using Kali Linux or DEFT Linux, for this chapter we will be using publicly-available, sample packet capture (`.pcap`) files that can be downloaded at `http://wiki.xplico.org/doku.php?id=pcap:pcap`.

The files needed are:

- **DNS**
- **MMS**
- **Webmail: Hotmail/Live**
- **HTTP (web)**
- **SIP example 1**

We will also require an SMTP sample file available from the Wireshark sample captures page at `https://wiki.wireshark.org/SampleCaptures`.

HTTP and web analysis using Xplico

In this exercise, we upload the HTTP (web)
(`xplico.org_sample_capture_web_must_use_xplico_nc.cfg.pcap`) sample packet
capture file.

For this HTTP analysis, we use Xplico to search for artifacts associated with the HTTP
protocol such as URLs, images from websites, and possible browser-related activities.

Once Xplico has been started, log in using the following credentials:

- **Username**: `xplico`
- **Password**: `xplico`

We then choose **New Case** from the menu on the left and select the **Uploading PCAP
capture file/s** button as we will be uploading files and not performing live captures or
acquisition. For each case we must also specify a **Case name**:

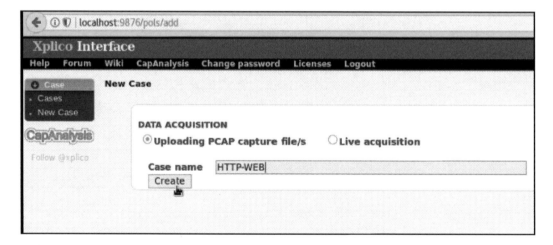

In the following screenshot, I have entered `HTTP-WEB` for the **Case name**. Click **Create** to
continue. The case **HTTPWEB** has now been created. Click **HTTPWEB** to continue to the
Session screen:

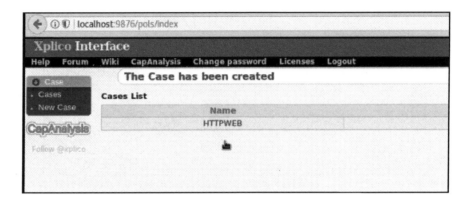

Now we create a new session for this instance of our case by clicking the **New Session** option in the menu to the left:

We give our session a name and click **Create** to continue:

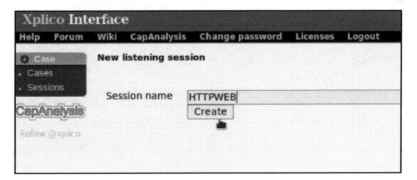

Our new session has been created with the name **HTTPWEB**:

Once our case and session details have been entered, we are presented with the main Xplico interface window, which displays the various categories of possible artifacts found, after our .pcap file has been uploaded and decoded including the HTTP, DNS, Web Mail and Facebook categories:

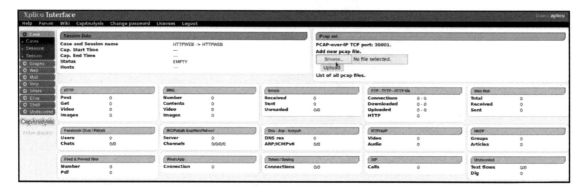

To upload our .pcap file, click the **Browse...** button in the **Pcap set** area to the top right, choose the downloaded
(xplico.org_sample_capture_web_must_use_xplico_nc.cfg.pcap) .pcap file and then click the **Upload** button to begin the decoding process in Xplico:

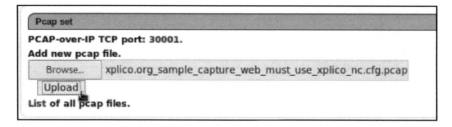

The decoding process can take a while depending on the size of the `.pcap` file as this process decodes the `.pcap` file into easily searchable categories within Xplico. Once finished, the **Status** field in the **Session Data** area reads **DECODING COMPLETED** and also displays the details of the **Case and Session name** and **Capture (Cap)** start and end times:

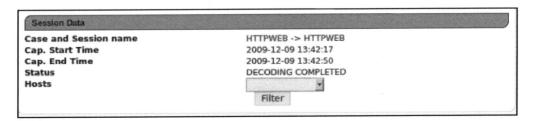

After the decoding is completed, the results are then displayed in the various category areas. In the following screenshot we can see that there is an entry in the **Undecoded** category under **Text flows**:

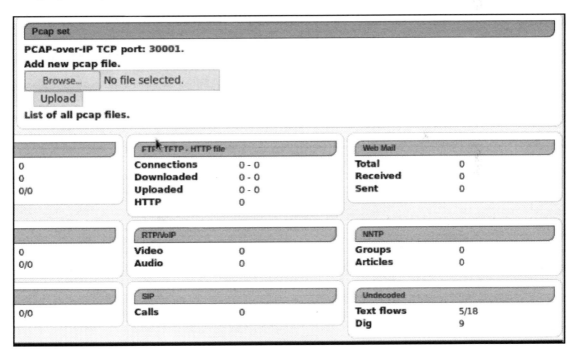

To analyze the decoded results, we use the menu to the extreme left of the Xplico interface. Seeing that we have results listed in the **Undecoded** category, click **Undecoded** in the menu, which expands into the **TCP-UDP** and **Dig** sub-menus. Click the **TCP-UDP** sub-menu to explore further:

The **TCP-UDP** option reveals destination IP, port, date and time, duration of connection, and an info file with more details. The destination IP entries marked in red can be clicked and also explored further:

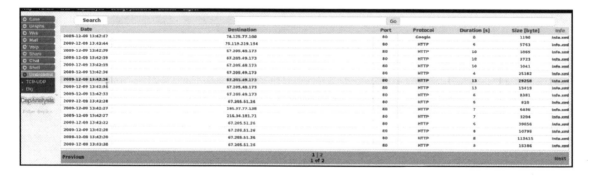

If we click the first destination IP entry, 74.125.77.100, we are prompted to save information details of this entry in a text file:

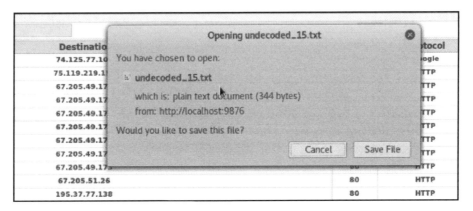

To view the contents of the file we can either open it directly from the saved location or use the cat command to display the contents within a Terminal by typing cat /root/Downloads/undecoded_15.txt:

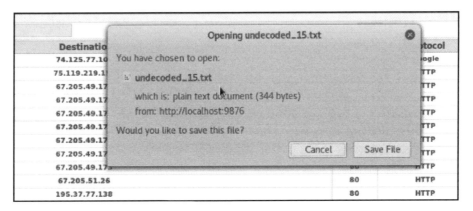

The results displayed in the previous Terminal window show that a .gif image was viewed or downloaded on Wed 09 December, 2009.

We can also click the `info.xml` link under the **Info** column to obtain more information:

Protocol	Duration [s]	Size [byte]	Info
Google	0	1190	info.xml pcap
HTTP	6	5763	info.xml
HTTP	10	1065	info.xml
HTTP	10	3723	info.xml

The **info.xml** shows the source and destination IP addresses and port numbers. We can now explore all destination IP addresses and their respective `info.xml` files to gather more information for our case:

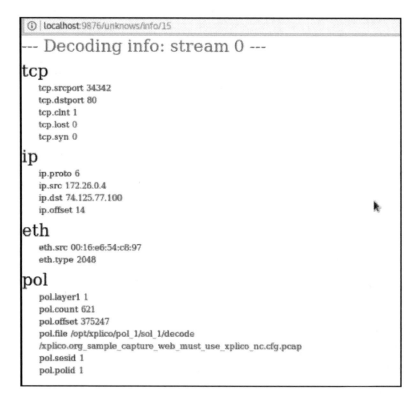

Let's go back to the **Undecoded** menu on the left and click the **Dig** sub-menu to explore our capture file further:

In the previous screenshot, the **Dig** sub-menu reveals several image artifacts in the form of .gif, .tif, and .jpg formats along with the dates viewed through an HTTP connection.

The images should be viewed and documented as part of our case findings:

Date	File
2009-12-09 13:42:48	file_15118910008.gif
2009-12-09 13:42:47	file_15118910007.gif
2009-12-09 13:42:40	file_15118910005.gif
2009-12-09 13:42:39	file_15118910006.gif
2009-12-09 13:42:27	file_15118910001.gif
2009-12-09 13:42:23	file_15118910003.jpg
2009-12-09 13:42:23	file_15118910004.tif
2009-12-09 13:42:22	file_15118910000.gif
2009-12-09 13:42:22	file_15118910002.gif

VoIP analysis using Xplico

Many organizations and even regular end users have implemented or used **VoIP (Voice over IP)** solutions mainly to reduce costs in voice and multimedia communication sessions that would have otherwise required the use of paid telephone lines. To use VoIP services we must use **SIP (Session Initiation Protocol)**.

For this exercise, we will be using the SIP example 1 (freeswitch4560_tosipphone_ok.pcap) packet capture file to analyze VoIP services, if any.

As with our previous HTTP web analysis, a new case and session must be created with the relevant details for this new case:

- **Case name**: SIP_Analysis
- **Session name**: Sip_File

Once the case and session has been created, browse to the .pcap file to be uploaded (freeswitch4560_tosipphone_ok.pcap) and click **Upload** to begin the decoding process:

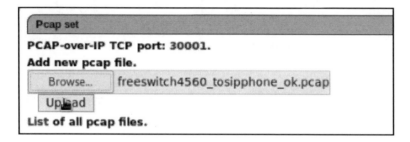

After the file has been decoded, we can see that there are **2** results listed in the **Calls** category in the lower right corner:

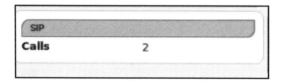

To begin exploring and analyzing the details of the VoIP calls, click the **VoIP** option on the menu to the left:

Clicking the **Sip** sub-menu, we are presented with details of the calls. We can see that calls were made from "Freeswitch" <sip:5555551212@192.168.1.111> to Freeswitch <sip:5555551212@192.168.1.112>:

From	To	Duration
"FreeSwitch" <sip:5555551212@192.168.1.111>	<sip:6580@192.168.1.12>	0:0:19
"FreeSwitch" <sip:5555551212@192.168.1.111>	<sip:6580@192.168.1.12>	0:0:0

Click on the **Duration** details (0 : 0 : 19) to analyze and explore further:

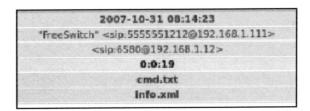

2007-10-31 08:14:23
"FreeSwitch" <sip:5555551212@192.168.1.111>
<sip:6580@192.168.1.12>
0:0:19
cmd.txt
info.xml

Let us first click on cmd.txt to view the information file and log:

In the previous screenshot, we can see details of the numbers in conversation, date, time, and duration. There is also an option to play the conversations on either end:

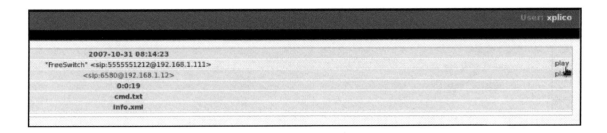

Email analysis using Xplico

Email uses different protocols to send and receive emails depending on the method used for sending, receiving, and storing/accessing emails. The three protocols used are:

- **Simple Mail Transfer Protocol (SMTP)**
- **Post Office Protocol (POP3)**
- **Internet Message Access Protocol (IMAP)**

SMTP uses port 25 and is used for sending emails.

POP3 uses port 110 and is used to retrieve emails by downloading them from the email server to the client. Microsoft Outlook is an example of a POP3 client.

IMAP4 uses port 143 and is similar to POP3 in that it retrieves email but leaves a copy of the email on the server and can be accessed anywhere through a web browser, commonly referred to as webmail. Gmail and Yahoo are examples of webmail.

For this exercise we will be using two sample files:

The first file is the **Webmail: Hotmail/Live** .pcap file (xplico.org_sample_capture_webmail_live.pcap), which can be downloaded from http://wiki.xplico.org/doku.php?id=pcap:pcap.

The second is the smtp.pcap file, which can be downloaded from https://wiki.wireshark.org/SampleCaptures.

For the analysis of the first .pcap file (**Webmail: Hotmail/Live**), I've created a case with the following details:

- **Case name**: Webmail_Analysis
- **Session name**: WebmailFile

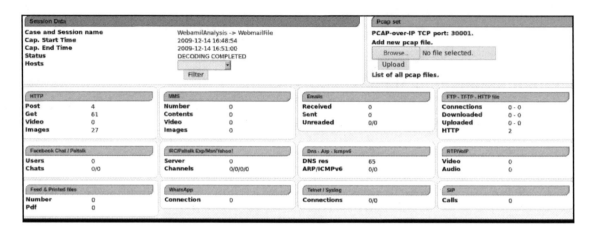

If we take a closer look at the decoded results we can see that we now have several populated categories including the HTTP, DNS -ARP - ICMP v6, and FTP - TFTP - HTTP file:

- **HTTP** category:

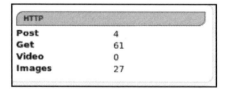

- **Dns -Arp - Icmpv6** category:

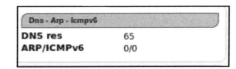

- **FTP - TFTP - HTTP** file:

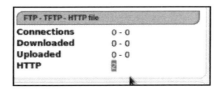

Now that we have an idea of what artifacts exist, let us now use the menu to the left side to analyze the results further.

Clicking the **Graphs** menu on the left displays domain information including the hostname, **CName (Canonical Name)** entries, IP addresses of the host, and also the info.xml files for each entry, for more detailed information of source and address:

Host	CName	IP	Info
spe.atdmt.com	spe.atdmt.com.edgesuite.net	194.224.66.90	info.xml pcap
rmd.atdmt.com	rmd.atdmt.com.edgesuite.net	194.224.66.83	info.xml
rmd.atdmt.com	rmd.atdmt.com.edgesuite.net		info.xml
spe.atdmt.com	spe.atdmt.com.edgesuite.net		info.xml
ads2.msads.net	msnads.vo.msecnd.net		info.xml
ads2.msads.net	msnads.vo.msecnd.net	65.54.81.78	info.xml

The `info.xml` file (as shown in the following screenshot) for the first entry
(`spe.atdmt.com`) reveals that a local IP (`ip.src`) of `10.0.2.15` is connected to the host
with an IP (`ip.dst`) of `194.179.1.100` (also illustrated in the previous screenshot of **IP**
field):

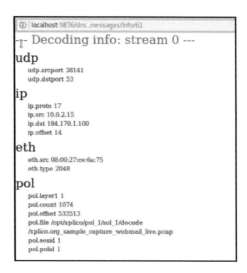

Next we move on to the **Web** menu and down to the **Site** sub-menu. A list of web pages
visited are displayed along with the date and time accessed. We can see the first three
entries belong to the domain `mail.live.com` and the fourth and fifth, `msn.com`:

We can examine the first **Site** entry by clicking on the `info.xml`. Under the HTTP section we can see that the Mozilla Firefox browser was used and the `sn118w.snt118.mail.live.com` host accessed:

Close the `info.xml` file and select the **Image** button, then click **Go** to display any images found:

The **Image** search results display several images and icons found. Click through the list to view the images:

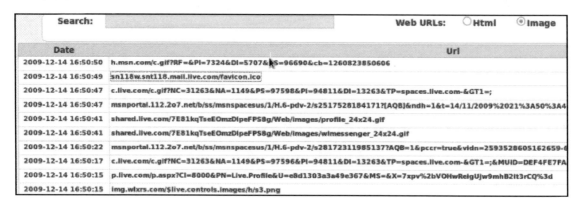

We can also view found images by returning to the **Web** menu to the left and then clicking the **Images** sub-menu. This presents us with a graphical grouping of the images with links to their respective pages also:

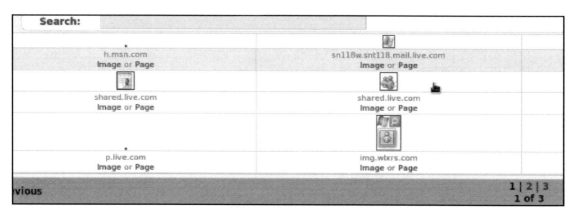

Moving down the main menu to the left, click the **Share** menu and then click the **HTTP file** sub-menu. Here we are presented with two items that we can investigate further by clicking their info.xml files:

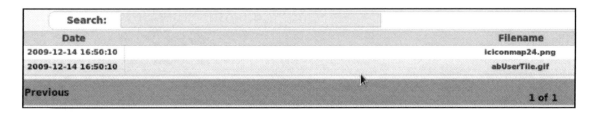

By clicking the `info.xml` file of the `abUserTile.gif`, we can see that this was accessed from host `194.224.66.18`:

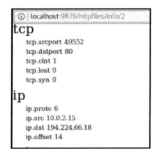

In the **Undecoded** menu and **HTTP** sub-menu we also have HTTP information about **Destination** IP `194.224.66.19`. Try exploring this further by clicking the `info.xml` file:

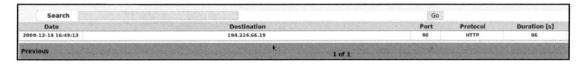

SMTP exercise using Wireshark sample file

For this example, we use the SMTP sample capture file downloaded from the Wireshark samples link at the beginning of this section.

I've created a case with the following details as seen in the **Session Data** section of the following screenshot:

- **Case name**: **SMTP**
- **Session name**: `SMTPfile`

Looking at the lower right corner of the screen we can see that there is an item in the
Unread field of the **Emails** category:

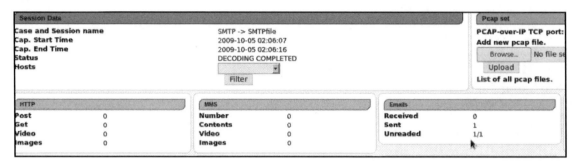

Knowing that we are analyzing and investigating emails, we can go directly to the **Mail**
menu and **Email** sub-menu on the left of the interface. This shows us that an email with no
subject was sent by `gurpartap@patriots.in` to `raj_deo2002in@yahoo.co.in`. Click
the **-(no subject)-** field to examine the email further:

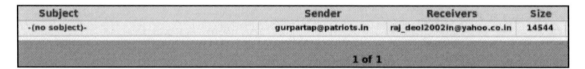

Subject	Sender	Receivers	Size
-(no subject)-	gurpartap@patriots.in	raj_deol2002in@yahoo.co.in	14544

1 of 1

After clicking the **-(no subject)-** field, we can now see the contents of the email:

Summary

I hope you enjoyed the exercises in this chapter as much as I did. Although some of us may have had difficulties in running Xplico due to updates and repository issues, I encourage you try Xplico on DEFT Linux 8.2 as Xplico can be a very useful GUI tool in decoding internet and network traffic. As we have seen and done in this chapter, Xplico can be used for HTTP, VoIP, and email analysis, but can also perform MMS, DNS, Facebook, and WhatsApp chat analysis. I encourage you try to download and analyze more sample files from the Xplico and Wireshark sample capture pages to become more familiar with analysis and examination using Xplico.

Let's move on to another all-in-one investigative tool now, the digital forensics framework, also known as **DFF**. See you in `Chapter 10`, *Revealing Evidence Using DFF*.

10
Revealing Evidence Using DFF

Welcome to the last chapter; you've made it. The final tool we'll be using is the **Digital Forensic Framework (DFF)**. DFF performs the automated analysis of images using a modular model all in one simple and user-friendly graphical user interface. DFF supports several image file formats including `.dd`, `.raw`, `.img`, `.bin`, E01, EWF, and AFF. Modules can be applied to view various file formats using embedded viewers for video, audio, PDFs, documents, images, and registry files.

The following are also supported by DFF:

- Browser history analysis
- File recovery
- Metadata and EXIF data analysis
- Memory/RAM analysis

Having all these features in one GUI allows for easy investigation and analysis of acquired images. For the exercises in this chapter, we'll be using images already acquired and available for download. This does not mean that we should use only one tool (such as DFF) for analysis. I recommend using at least two tools for all investigative tasks so that the results can be compared, adding to the accuracy and integrity of the investigation.

 Remember, when acquiring your own images, always ensure that the integrity of the device and evidence is maintained through the use of write-blockers and the use of hashing tools. It's also important that we only work with forensic copies of the evidence unless circumstances require otherwise to again preserve the evidence.

Let's take a look at the topics we will be covering in this chapter:

- Installing DFF
- Starting the DFF GUI
- Recovering deleted files with DFF
- File analysis with DFF

Installing DFF

To carry out investigations using DFF, we first require the Kali Linux 2016.1 ISO image. I've chosen to use the 64-bit version and also have it running as a virtual host within VirtualBox.

The Kali Linux 2016.1 ISO image can be downloaded from the `https://www.kali.org/downloads/`:

1. Once Kali 2016.1 is installed as a virtual host, we can use the `uname -a` command to view the version details:

```
root@kali:~# uname -a
Linux kali 4.3.0-kali1-amd64 #1 SMP Debian 4.3.3-5kali4 (2016-01-13) x86_64 GNU/Linux
root@kali:~#
```

2. To begin installing DFF, we first need to update the `sources.list` with the repository used in Kali Sana. Although we browsed directly to the `sources.list` file in the previous chapter, here are two additional ways in which we can also perform this task using the Terminal.

   In a new Terminal, we can type the following:

   ```
   echo "deb http://old.kali.org/kali sana main non-free
   contrib" >
   /etc/apt/sources.list
   ```

```
root@kali:~# echo "deb http://old.kali.org/kali sana main non-free contrib" > /etc/apt/sources.list
```

Alternatively, we can instead use the second method by typing the following:

nano /etc/apt/sources.list

```
root@kali:~# nano /etc/apt/sources.list
```

Followed by the details of the repositories:

```
deb http://http.kali.org/kali kali-rolling main contrib
non-free
deb src http://http.kali.org/kali kali-rolling main contrib
non-free
deb http://http.kali.org/kali sana main contrib
```

3. Then, press *Ctrl + X* to exit, and press *Y* to save the changes to the sources.list file:

```
Save modified buffer?  (Answering "No" will DISCARD changes.)
Y Yes
N No              ^C Cancel
```

4. Next, we update Kali by typing apt-get update:

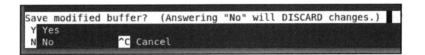

```
File  Edit  View  Search  Terminal  Help
root@kali:~# echo "deb http://old.kali.org/kali sana main non-free contrib" > /e
tc/apt/sources.list
root@kali:~# apt-get update
Get:1 http://old.kali.org/kali sana InRelease [20.3 kB]
Get:2 http://old.kali.org/kali sana/main amd64 Packages [12.8 MB]
Get:3 http://old.kali.org/kali sana/non-free amd64 Packages [163 kB]
Get:4 http://old.kali.org/kali sana/contrib amd64 Packages [87.7 kB]
Fetched 13.1 MB in 11s (1,107 kB/s)
Reading package lists... Done
root@kali:~#
```

5. Now, we install the Advanced Forensics Format Library by typing:

```
apt-get install libafflib0
```

```
root@kali:~# apt-get install libafflib0
Reading package lists... Done
Building dependency tree
Reading state information... Done
The following packages were automatically installed and are no longer required:
  libavdevice-ffmpeg56 libavfilter-ffmpeg5 libpff1 libpgm-5.1-0 libphonon4
  libtre5 libzmq3 phonon phonon-backend-vlc python-apsw python-magic
  python-qt4-phonon
Use 'apt autoremove' to remove them.
The following additional packages will be installed:
  libssl1.0.0
The following packages will be REMOVED:
  afflib-tools autopsy bulk-extractor dff kali-linux-full libafflib0v5
  libtsk13 sleuthkit
The following NEW packages will be installed:
  libafflib0 libssl1.0.0
0 upgraded, 2 newly installed, 8 to remove and 11 not upgraded.
Need to get 1,264 kB of archives.
After this operation, 25.8 MB disk space will be freed.
Do you want to continue? [Y/n] y
```

As shown in the preceding screenshot, press *Y* to continue. This is a somewhat lengthy process as it installs components for several forensic tools including Autopsy, Sleuthkit, Bulk_extractor, and DFF, as shown in the following screenshot:

```
Do you want to continue? [Y/n] y
Get:1 http://old.kali.org/kali sana/main amd64 libssl1.0.0 amd64 1.0.1k-3 [1,037
 kB]
Get:2 http://old.kali.org/kali sana/main amd64 libafflib0 amd64 3.7.5-1 [227 kB]
Fetched 1,264 kB in 1s (754 kB/s)
Preconfiguring packages ...
(Reading database ... 298942 files and directories currently installed.)
Removing kali-linux-full (2016.1.0) ...
Removing afflib-tools (3.7.7-3) ...
Removing autopsy (2.24-1.1) ...
Removing bulk-extractor (1.5.3+git20150907-0kali1+b1) ...
Removing dff (1.3.0+dfsg.1-4.1+kali1+b1) ...
Removing sleuthkit (4.2.0-3) ...
Removing libtsk13 (4.2.0-3) ...
Removing libafflib0v5 (3.7.7-3) ...
Processing triggers for man-db (2.7.5-1) ...
Processing triggers for gnome-menus (3.13.3-6) ...
Processing triggers for desktop-file-utils (0.22-1) ...
Processing triggers for mime-support (3.59) ...
Processing triggers for menu (2.1.47) ...
Processing triggers for libc-bin (2.21-6) ...
Selecting previously unselected package libssl1.0.0:amd64.
(Reading database ... 298106 files and directories currently installed.)
Preparing to unpack .../libssl1.0.0_1.0.1k-3_amd64.deb ...
Unpacking libssl1.0.0:amd64 (1.0.1k-3) ...
Selecting previously unselected package libafflib0.
Preparing to unpack .../libafflib0_3.7.5-1_amd64.deb ...
Unpacking libafflib0 (3.7.5-1) ...
Setting up libssl1.0.0:amd64 (1.0.1k-3) ...
Setting up libafflib0 (3.7.5-1) ...
Processing triggers for libc-bin (2.21-6) ...
root@kali:~#
```

6. Once the library has been successfully installed, we can install DFF by typing the following:

```
apt-get install dff
```

```
root@kali:~#
root@kali:~# apt-get install dff
Reading package lists... Done
Building dependency tree
Reading state information... Done
The following packages were automatically installed and are no longer required:
  libavdevice-ffmpeg56 libavfilter-ffmpeg5 libdate-manip-perl libpgm-5.1-0
  libzmq3
Use 'apt autoremove' to remove them.
The following additional packages will be installed:
  libavcodec56 libavdevice55 libavformat56 libavresample2 libavutil54 libicu52
  libswscale3 libvpx1 libx264-142
Recommended packages:
  hal
The following NEW packages will be installed:
  dff libavcodec56 libavdevice55 libavformat56 libavresample2 libavutil54
  libicu52 libswscale3 libvpx1 libx264-142
0 upgraded, 10 newly installed, 0 to remove and 11 not upgraded.
Need to get 16.4 MB of archives.
After this operation, 62.4 MB of additional disk space will be used.
Do you want to continue? [Y/n]
```

7. Press *Y* to continue when prompted to allow the installation of DFF 1.3.3 to continue:

```
Processing triggers for mime-support (3.59) ...
Setting up libavutil54:amd64 (6:11.3-1+deb8u1) ...
Setting up libavresample2:amd64 (6:11.3-1+deb8u1) ...
Setting up libvpx1:amd64 (1.3.0-3) ...
Setting up libx264-142:amd64 (2:0.142.2431+gita5831aa-1+b2) ...
Setting up libavcodec56:amd64 (6:11.3-1+deb8u1) ...
Setting up libavformat56:amd64 (6:11.3-1+deb8u1) ...
Setting up libavdevice55:amd64 (6:11.3-1+deb8u1) ...
Setting up libicu52:amd64 (52.1-8) ...
Setting up libswscale3:amd64 (6:11.3-1+deb8u1) ...
Setting up dff (1.3.0+dfsg.1-4.1+kali1) ...
Processing triggers for libc-bin (2.21-6) ...
Processing triggers for menu (2.1.47) ...
root@kali:~#
```

8. To ensure that DFF has been successfully installed, we can type dff in the Terminal, which loads the available modules within DFF:

```
root@kali:~# dff
loading modules in /usr/lib/python2.7/dist-packages/dff/modules
[OK]    loading man v1.0.0
[OK]    loading history v1.0.0
[OK]    loading show_cwd v1.0.0
[OK]    loading find v1.2.0
[OK]    loading cd v1.0.0
```

Once the Welcome on Digital Forensics Framework banner is displayed, this means that our DFF installation was successful. We can now begin our investigation by running the DFF GUI:

```
[OK]    loading cut v1.0.0
[OK]    loading split v1.0.0

#########################################
# Welcome on Digital Forensics Framework #
#########################################

dff / > █
```

Starting the DFF GUI

Now that we have DFF installed, we can first verify the version of DFF and also view some of the commands within DFF, using the CLI:

1. To view the version of DFF installed, in a new Terminal, type dff -v. In the following screenshot, we can see that the version is 1.3.0:

```
root@kali:~# dff -v
dff version 1.3.0
```

2. To view the available options, we type dff -h:

```
root@kali:~#
root@kali:~# dff -h
DFF
Digital Forensic Framework

Usage: /usr/bin/dff [options]
Options:
   -v       --version              display current version
   -g       --graphical            launch graphical interface
   -b       --batch=FILENAME       executes batch contained in FILENAME
   -l       --language=LANG        use LANG as interface language
   -h       --help                 display this help message
   -d       --debug                redirect IO to system console
            --verbosity=LEVEL      set verbosity level when debugging [0-3]
   -c       --config=FILEPATH      use config file from FILEPATH

root@kali:~#
```

3. To launch the graphical interface, we type dff -g:

```
root@kali:~# dff -g
```

4. The graphical interface can also be started by clicking on
   Applications | Forensics | dff gui:

5. Once opened using either method, we are then presented with the DFF GUI:

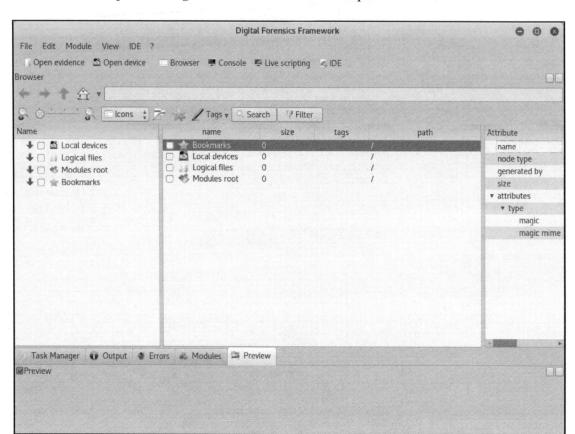

Recovering deleted files with DFF

For this exercise, we'll be using a very small .raw image created using DD. This file is approximately 6 MB and is publicly available at http://dftt.sourceforge.net/test7/index.html:

1. Click on the ZIP file to download it and extract it to its default location. When extracted, the name of the file shows up as 7-ntfs-undel.dd. Using the preceding steps, start DD if you haven't yet opened the program. Before we import the image, take a moment to observe the icons next to the entries in the main window area. The icon for the **Logical files** field is a white folder with a hint of blue:

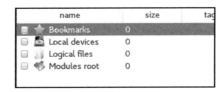

When we add an image in the following steps, a blue plus sign will appear over the folder icon.

2. To open our downloaded DD image in DFF, either click on **File | Open evidence** or click on the Open evidence button, as shown in the following screenshot:

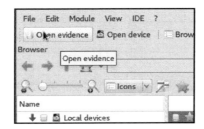

3. In the **Select evidence type** box, ensure that the **RAW format** option is checked and the **File** option is selected in the drop-down box. Click on the green plus (+) sign to browse to the 7-ntfs-undel.dd file. Click **OK** to continue:

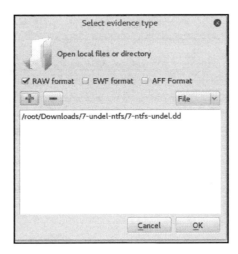

In both the left pane and the main windows of DFF, observe the plus sign next to the **Logical files** icon. This tells us that although there are no entries for **size**, **tags**, and **path**, the image has been successfully added and we can explore the **Logical files** section:

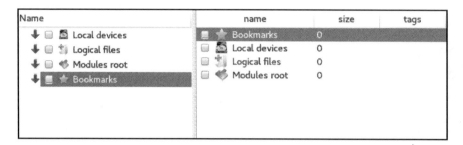

4. In the left window pane, click on the **Logical files** category. In the main window, the name of the image is displayed:

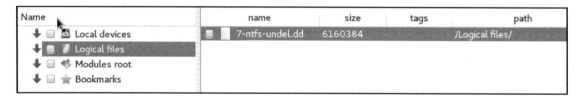

5. Double-click on the name of the image in the main window. In the **Apply module** box, click on **Yes**:

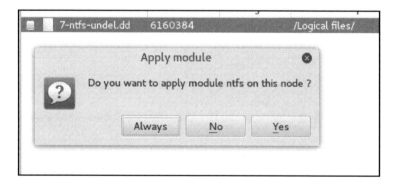

After the module is applied, the image name appears (`7-ntfs-undel.dd`) under **Logical files** in the left pane:

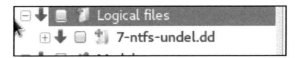

6. Click on the plus sign to the left of the image name in the left pane to expand the menu and view the contents image. Once expanded, we can see that there are two folders, namely `NTFS` and `NTFS unallocated`:

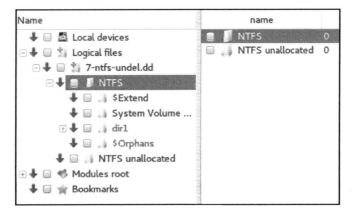

 Entries marked in red (`dir1` and `$Orphans`) are deleted files.

7. To view the contents of the files, double-click on the NTFS entry in the main window:

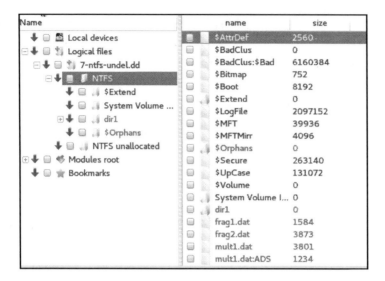

8. Click on the frag1.dat deleted file. The right pane displays information about the file including the following:
   - **name:** frag1.dat
   - **node type:** file deleted
   - **generated by:** ntfs
   - **Creation time:** 2004-02-29 20:00:17
   - **File accessed time:** 2004-02-29 20:00:17
   - **File altered time:** 2004-02-29 20:00:17
   - **MFT altered time:** 2004-02-29 20:00:17

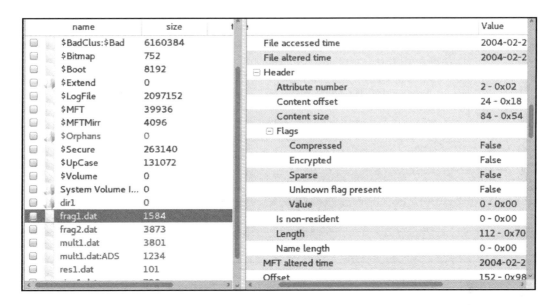

9. Let's inspect another deleted file. Click on the `mult1.dat:ADS` stream and view its details:

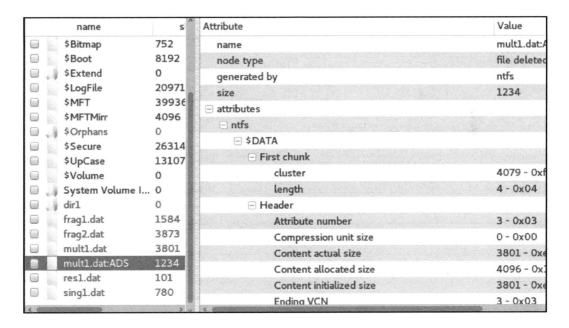

According to the file listing at `http://dftt.sourceforge.net/test7/index.html`, this image contains 11 deleted files, including `mult1.dat:ADS`, which contains hidden content in an NTFS Alternate Data Stream. DFF has found all 11 files. Visit the preceding site or view the following screenshot to view the names of the deleted files for comparison:

Name	Size	MD5	Note
\res1.dat	101	9036637712b491904cd0bfbdbe648453	Resident file (data is stored in MFT entry and not in a cluster)
\sing1.dat	780	59b20779f69ff9f0ac5fcd2c38835a79	single cluster file
\mult1.dat	3801	ffd27bd782bdce67750b6b9ee069d2ef	multiple cluster, non-fragmented file
\mult1.dat:ADS	1234	ba1b9eedb1c091ddca253d35dde8f616	multiple cluster, second data attribute (Alternate Data Stream)
\frag1.dat	1584	7a3bc5b763bef201202108f4ba128149	fragmented file
\frag2.dat	3873	0e80ab84ef0087e60dfc67b88a1cf13e	fragmented file with frag1.dat mixed in
\dir1\	1024	N/A	directory
\dir1\mult2.dat	1715	59cf0e9cd107bc1e75afb7374f6e05bb	multiple cluster, non-fragmented in deleted directory
\dir1\dir2\	1024	N/A	directory in deleted directory
\dir1\dir2\frag3.dat	2027	21121699487f3fbbdb9a4b3391b6d3e0	fragmented file in deleted directories
\dir3\sing2.dat	1005	c229626f6a71b167ad7e50c4f2fccdb1	single cluster file in a directory whose MFT entry has been reallocated (to res1.dat)

File analysis with DFF

Now that we've looked at the file recovery process, let's continue our investigation with DFF by examining an image file with more content.

For this exercise, we will be using another publicly available image called the *JPEG Search Test #1 (Jun '04)*. The ZIP file can be downloaded at `http://dftt.sourceforge.net/test8/index.html`:

1. After downloading the ZIP file, extract it to its default location. The name of the decompressed file is `8-jpeg-search.dd`.
2. Open the evidence file in DFF by repeating the steps in the preceding exercise:
   1. Start DFF by clicking on **Applications** | **Forensics** | **ddf gui**.
   2. Click on the **Open evidence** button.
   3. Browse to the `8-jpeg-search.dd` image file (as seen in the following screenshot).

4. Click **OK:**

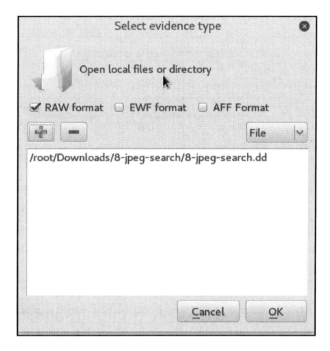

3. Click on **Logical files** in the left pane and then double-click on the filename (8-jpeg-search.dd) in the main window:

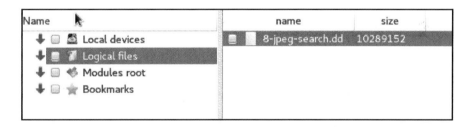

4. In the **Apply module** box, choose **Yes** when prompted to apply the NTFS module on the node:

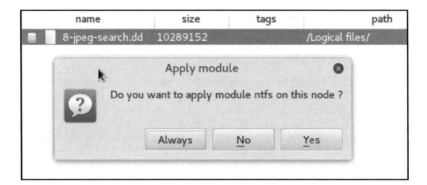

5. Click on the plus sign (+) in the left pane, next to **Logical files,** to expand the menu.
6. Click on the plus sign (+) next to the filename, 8-jpeg-search.dd, to expand the menu.

   In this exercise, we are also presented with two found NTFS folders named NTFS and NTFS unallocated:

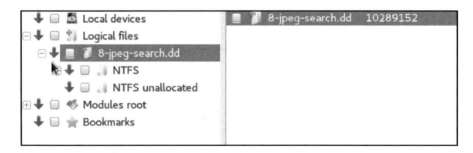

7. Click on NTFS in the left pane to view the subfolders and files (displayed in the main window):

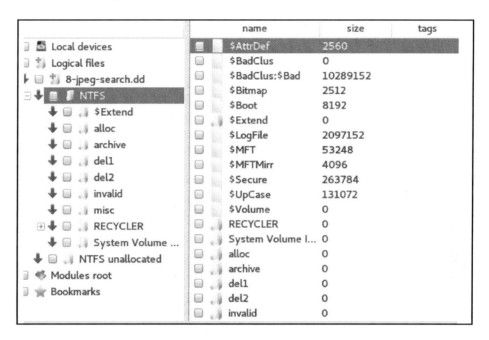

8. Click on the alloc folder to view its contents. Within the alloc folder, there are two files with colorful icons in the main window:
   - file1.jpg
   - file2.dat

9. Click on file1.jpg if it isn't already selected:

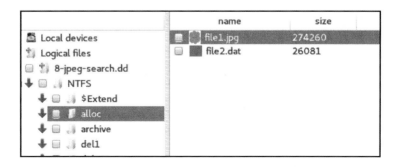

10. In the **Attribute** column to the right, scroll down to the **type** field. Note the following attribute values, as seen in the following screenshot:
    - **magic**: **JPEG image data, JFIF standard 1.01**
    - **magic mime**: **image/jpeg**

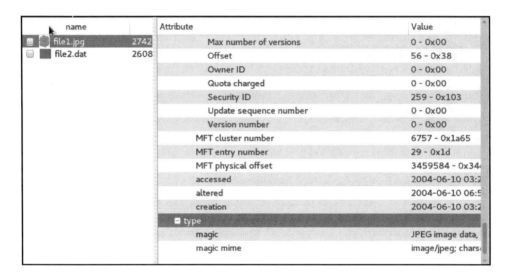

11. Double-click on `file1.jpg` and click on **Yes** when prompted to apply the pictures module on the node, which will allow us to view the image:

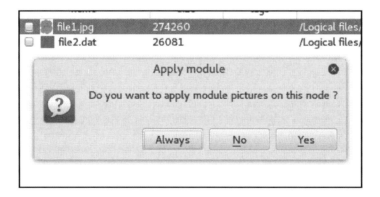

The preview window opens, showing the image with the file path under the image as `/Logical files/8-jpeg-search.dd/NTFS/alloc/file1.jpg`:

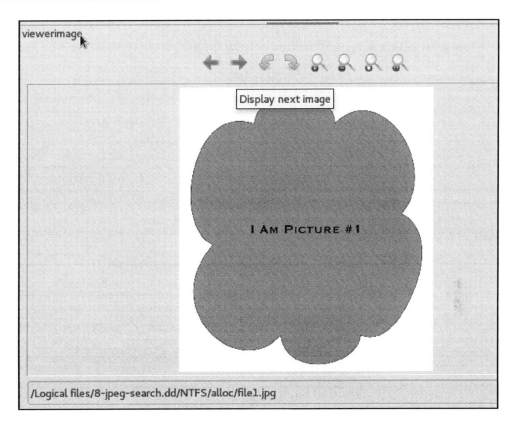

viewerimage

Display next image

I AM PICTURE #1

/Logical files/8-jpeg-search.dd/NTFS/alloc/file1.jpg

12. Return to the DFF browser interface by clicking on the **Browser** button under the **Open evidence** button:

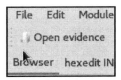

File   Edit   Module

Open evidence

Browser   hexedit IN

13. Click on `file2.dat` and scroll down to the **type** attribute and note the **magic** and **magic mime** values:
   - **magic: JPEG image data, JFIF standard 1.01**
   - **magic mime: image/jpeg**

Note that even though the extension of `file2` is `.dat`, DFF has read the header and has listed the true type of the file as a JPEG/JFIF file:

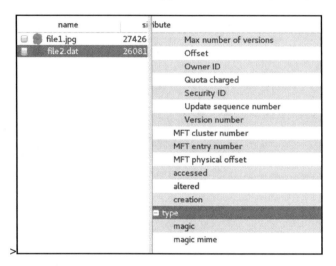

14. Double-click on `file2.dat` in the `alloc` folder (under the `file1.jpg` file) and click on **Yes** when prompted to apply the pictures module:

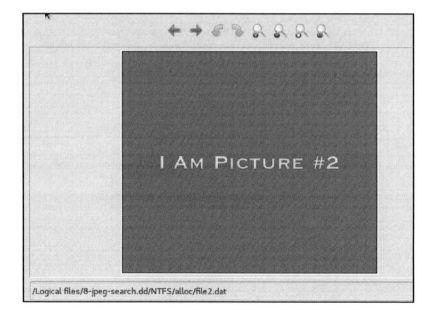

15. Click on the **Browse** button to return to the DFF interface. Click on the `del1` folder in the left-pane to explore its contents. Inside the `del1` folder is a single file named `file6.jpg`, listed as deleted in the **Attributes** column, as seen in the following screenshot. Noteworthy values in the **Attributes** column include:

- **name**: `file6.jpg`
- **node type**: **deleted**
- **magic**: **JPEG image data, JFIF standard.**
- **magic mime**: **image/jpeg;**

16. Double-click on the `file6.jpg` and apply the module to preview the file (be sure to click on the **Browser** button to return to the DFF browser interface):

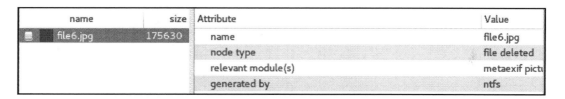

name	size	Attribute	Value
file6.jpg	175630	name	file6.jpg
		node type	file deleted
		relevant module(s)	metaexif pict
		generated by	ntfs

17. Click on the `del2` folder in the left pane. The main window shows a single file with a peculiar extension named `file7.hmm`. The **Attribute** column lists the file as deleted; however, the **type** attribute shows the following:

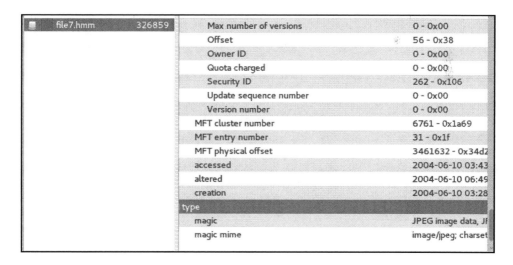

file7.hmm	326859		
		Max number of versions	0 - 0x00
		Offset	56 - 0x38
		Owner ID	0 - 0x00
		Quota charged	0 - 0x00
		Security ID	262 - 0x106
		Update sequence number	0 - 0x00
		Version number	0 - 0x00
		MFT cluster number	6761 - 0x1a69
		MFT entry number	31 - 0x1f
		MFT physical offset	3461632 - 0x34d2
		accessed	2004-06-10 03:43
		altered	2004-06-10 06:49
		creation	2004-06-10 03:28
		type	
		magic	JPEG image data, JF
		magic mime	image/jpeg; charset

18. Double-click on the `file7.hmm` file and apply the picture module to preview the `.jpg` image:

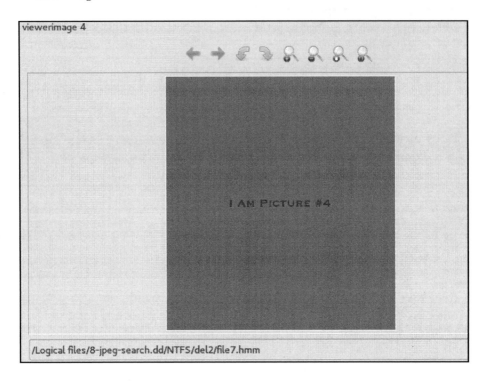

Summary

Congratulations, you made it to the end. In this final chapter, we looked at the very versatile DFF. Using DFF, we performed file recovery, folder exploration, file analysis, and were also able to preview files using various modules.

It's important to remember that although DFF can perform several tasks, other tools used in previous chapters should be used to verify the accuracy of the findings. It's also important to document your steps as you progress through the investigation in the event that you must recreate the investigative process or retrace your steps.

On behalf of myself, the reviewers, the editors, and the entire Packt family, thank you for purchasing this book. Be sure to have a look at the many other excellent titles available at `https://www.packtpub.com/`.